# The Modern Witch's Guide to Magic and Spells

D0884964

Other Books by Sarah Lyddon Morrison

*The Modern Witch's Spellbook*
*The Modern Witch's Spellbook: Book II*
*The Modern Witch's Dreambook*
*The Modern Witch's Book of Home Remedies*
*The Modern Witch's Book of Symbolism*

# The Modern Witch's Guide to Magic and Spells

SARAH LYDDON MORRISON

CITADEL PRESS
Kensington Publishing Corp.
www.kensingtonbooks.com

CITADEL PRESS books are published by

Kensington Publishing Corp.
850 Third Avenue
New York, NY 10022

All Kensington titles, imprints, and distributed lines are available at special quantity discounts for bulk purchases for sales promotions, premiums, fund raising, educational, or institutional use. Special book excerpts or customized printings can also be created to fit specific needs. For details, write or phone the office of the Kensington special sales manager: Kensington Publishing Corp., 850 Third Avenue, New York, NY 10022, attn: Special Sales Department, phone 1-800-221-2647.

Kensington and the K logo Reg. U.S. Pat. & TM Office
Citadel Press is a trademark of Kensington Publishing Corp.

First printing  1998

10 9 8 7 6 5 4

Printed in the United States of America

Library of Congress Cataloging-in-Publication Data

Morrison, Sarah Lyddon.
    The modern witch's guide to magic and spells / Sarah Lyddon Morrison.
        p.  cm.
    "A Citadel Press book."
    ISBN 0–8065–1963–0 (pbk.)
    1. Witchcraft.   I. Title.
    BF1566.M75   1998
    133.4′3—dc21                                          97–45629
                                                              CIP

To James Earl Butler,
who has bewitched me for twenty years.
He's my inspiration and the love of my life.

# Contents

# Introduction

WITH THIS BOOK, the third in my series on witchcraft, I take us on a coast-to-coast journey in search of the arts. I traveled to Hawaii twice this year to study Huna, the ancient Hawaiian knowledge of the sciences, part of which was the study of sorcery. Kahunas practiced the arts of the Huna, and I use their prayers to invoke the ancient sorcery of the Hawaiian people.

Huna sorcery is practiced exactly as Western sorcery was practiced in ancient times. I have no idea why European sorcery and the magic of the Pacific should be identical in the particulars of how they're practiced. But they are identical, and it's this ancient tradition that I tell you about in this volume and in the *Modern Witch's Spellbook I* and *II*. The sorcery I speak of is authentic, not the modern Wicca religion that is an entirely different branch of magic. In fact Wiccans don't understand the tradition I speak of and have written me some nasty letters out of ignorance. I hope these will stop and that Wiccans can realize the world is big enough to accommodate many ideas about magic, not just their own as the one true religion. I don't practice a witchcraft religion with this sorcery, and you do not need to belong to a coven to practice it. All you need are the ingredients for the spells and the natural extrasensory perception ability you need to cast spells.

The other tradition I explore in this book was researched in South Carolina, a hotbed of Obeah and African magic. I went there on a research trip and found a treasure of magical practices that I bring to this work in the form of spells and superstitions. Obeah was the province of the Africans brought to this country as slaves; it took the form of Voodoo in Louisiana and Haiti, and plain Obeah in the Caribbean Islands, Brazil, and South Carolina, as well as elsewhere in the South. Charleston was my destination, and I received a lot of help from the South Carolina Historical Society, which opened its collections to me to research the magical works I present in this book. So I traveled from coast to coast to put this book together for you, and it's a much more sophisticated work than the other two books, reflecting my advancing age and interests.

This book contains some dark magic, unlike the second book, which contained not a shred. Since I wrote that second book, I've decided that authentic magical works cannot ignore the desire to protect oneself from evil witchcraft and, on occasion, to practice a bit of the black art as well. We sometimes have enemies who need to be put in their place. I do not wish you to harm anyone very much with the darker spells, as it may be that they'll backfire and harm you instead. I put them in for advanced witches who have gained enough knowledge to successfully cast a dark spell.

The method of casting spells is a bit complex. It's the traditional sorcerer's method in the West, and the Kahuna's method in the Pacific. Here is how it's done: While chanting a spell, concentrate with the utmost emotion and ESP on the person you're casting your spell, and send the spell with an overwhelming moment of emotion and ESP at the person. You must not waiver in your concentration on the person and on the emotion you've conjured from within, and you should do your spells by yourself as you'll probably have to shout the words to get their full effect. Hold the image of the person you're bewitching for a minute in your mind's eye after casting the spell, and continue to send waves of ESP emotion at the image. Now and again, for about an hour after casting the spell, picture the person with the spell accomplished on him to solidify the effect.

The traditions of East and West come together in this method of spell casting, and you need a pictorial mind to be a witch. You must be able to visualize the object of your spell clearly, otherwise it will have no effect whatsoever. If you've done it correctly, your spell will work. Hundreds of my readers tell me my spells have helped them, and I expect the workers of the charms in this book will have the same report.

*Note to my readers*: Witchcraft spells can and do work and are serious business. Don't use them for frivolous reasons or with hatred in your heart. They can and do backfire. An example of my most recent backfire was when I put a spell on my boss to get her to change jobs. Within one month of doing the spell on her, *I* left the organization and am in an entirely new place (a good one, I might add) in my life. This happened to be a successful backfire, but others can prove disastrous and cause you no end of pain. Study the occult with care. Only experienced witches should try the more difficult procedures in this book.

# Part I

## BACKGROUND

## *Are You a Witch?*

HOW DO YOU KNOW if you're a witch, a reader has asked me. Well, it's a complex subject and one that should be covered by me in this book.

You're a witch if you experienced extrasensory perception as a child or young adult, can foretell the future, do psychokinesis, or perform one of the other arts associated with ESP. Extrasensory perception is in all of us in varying degrees. If a child is encouraged to use it, then the ESP lingers. If not, then the talent leaves. My mother encouraged me when I was a child, and I was able to foretell some events. I have olfactory ESP, which is very rare. It means that when I'm having an ESP event, I get this internal odor that comes close to smelling like old metal, and it permeates my body. Then within a week of having the event, someone I know dies.

So ESP is the first sign that you're a witch. A broad interest in the world of the unseen is another indication that you'd make a good witch. If you believe that there's a lot more to life going on than what you can see, taste, smell, feel, or hear, then you're ripe for witchcraft. You can tell I'm interested by the books I write. Dream interpretation, home remedies, symbols—all these are related subjects to witchcraft. And witchcraft is just a generic term with me, as there's no better way of expressing the concept of the occult as I practice it.

Sorcery is too western a concept for the witchcraft I espouse. I believe that African Obeah works very well, and that the gypsy and American Indian witchcraft work too. Hawaiian magic is very powerful, and the arts of Polynesia have only been scratched on the surface.

But if you believe in God, there's no problem with practicing witchcraft as I present it. Many people feel you can't believe in Jesus Christ and believe in witchcraft. It's true that the Bible admonishes against the practice of sorcery, but this isn't the sorcery using Grimoires and human sacrifices that the Bible really is talking about.

So a belief in God, and a strong one, is part of being a witch. I've adjusted my concept of God as I've grown, and now find Him a loving God who takes you or leaves you if you don't believe in Him. So my current concept of God is that you must have a strong belief in Him to reap the rewards of belief. This goes for Christ, too. I'm a Christian, and I know a lot of people aren't, but I believe Christ rules with God and is part of Him.

The concept of evil spells arises. I don't believe you should harm anyone unless the provocation is really extreme. Then it's better to put a spell on someone than it is to murder them. So if you're in a situation where murder is an option, then by all means use a black spell. It will accomplish the same end without getting you in deep kimchee.

So to be a witch, you should have ESP and be interested in the world of the unseen. You should believe strongly in God, and you might even pray that your spells work.

## For Disbelievers

I received a letter from an irate young woman. She had tried a spell and it didn't work. How could I claim they worked, she asked.

There's a lot more to making a spell work than trying it and expecting it to work. You have to go through a very specific process that takes quite a bit of practice to accomplish so it's just right.

For example—there's the spell itself. You have to chant this with a huge amount of emotion in your voice. It doesn't do to chant a spell in a wimpy voice. Only the highest amount of emotion will work, and you have to be able to cast the emotion (whether love or hate) through your body to the image in your head or, sometimes, to your arm, down through your fingers, and out into the object.

And you have to be able to visualize the object of your spell, which requires that you have a visual mind. If you can't visualize a face clearly, then you can't do spells. It's as simple as that.

So you must be able to visualize the object of your spell, chant the spell with huge emotion, throw your emotion at the visualized conjuration, and do all these things at the same time. This is not easy; it takes practice.

First you must practice visualizing, then summoning emotion to cast. Then, practice casting emotion at your visual image, and practice throwing emotion down your left hand and out your fingers. Then memorize the spell you want to do so you're not referring to a book at the time of the conjuration.

Another aspect of casting spells is the amount of ESP you use. You need to practice ESP and use it to cast your spell, as you're not only casting it at the visual image you create, but at the actual person in the image. So you need to get a book on ESP and study how to use your ability.

But the people who laugh at us because we practice witchcraft are the subject here. They must be shown that witchcraft does work. If you do the following spell on someone—and it works—show the person this page and tell her that she was the object of your spell, and that it does, in fact, work. Then you'll have made a believer out of a disbeliever.

So here's a little spell to make disbelievers believe in witchcraft. It is meant to have the person greet you with a kiss the next time she sees you. Chances are she doesn't ordinarily do this, so it's a real test.

Take a red lipstick and draw a lip print on a piece of white parchment paper. Then take a red candle and burn the parchment while chanting:

> *Kiss me when we meet,*
> *Kiss me,* [mention the person's name]
> *Greet me with your lips*
> *And say you missed me.*
> *But most of all kiss me.*

When the person runs up to you and kisses you when you meet, pull out this page and show it to her. She will be amazed that the spell worked. Don't forget to visualize, conjure love, and cast the spell in the proper way.

### On Becoming Wiccan

I have a reader who is debating whether or not to become a Wiccan. She has a Pagan boyfriend, and he's influencing her to become a Wiccan.

Wicca is the witchcraft that you hear the most about these days. It's a nature religion and, I feel, believes it's the one true faith. I've never met a ruder, more self-righteous bunch of people in my life. I would have nothing to do with the Wiccans if I were you.

I've received many letters from Wiccans over the years, and they are so ignorant that they do not even realize that the brand of witchcraft I write about is an ancient belief predating theirs. They think that my witchcraft is phony and doesn't work, that I try to promote beliefs (which I don't), and that in general I have no right to be writing my books.

This book is different than my other two spell books as it discusses Obeah and Hawaiian magic as well as some French spells, but it is authentic magic in every way and, I can assure you, the beliefs that it represents predate Wiccan beliefs. African magic is as old as time, and Hawaiian magic goes back to the Stone Age.

To my young reader who has talents that would make her an excellent modern witch, I'd like to say she should develop them. She has lucid dreams that come true a lot of the time, and she can walk into a room and tell people what they're feeling and why—and she feels inhabited by spirits from time to time. Such talents should make her an excellent sorcerer and, therefore, modern witch. She should try concentrating on visual images and sending telepathic messages to her images. She could do this without practicing witchcraft just to exercise her ability. When trying out my powers, I used to influence the outcomes of pool games by concentrating on the pool ball of my opponent and seeing to it that it missed the pocket.

I learned this pool game trick from a Kahuna in Hawaii who taught me to concentrate my powers. After practicing concentration for a while, I killed a bee by concentrating on it. I willed it to die, and it did. You can influence objects by learning to concentrate on them, and you practice witchcraft the same way by visualizing and throwing emotion at the visualization.

But I would recommend that you do not join a group of other witches and practice the craft, as their beliefs only muddy the waters of what actually takes place when casting a spell. If you must believe in something, believe in God and, if you've had a Christian upbringing, in His son, Jesus Christ. Christianity frowns on the practice of witchcraft, but that is mostly the Wiccan variety of groups of witches who meet and carry on in the nude, have ceremonies for the devil, and so forth. If I were a religion I'd frown on that, too. But using your God-given talents is not a crime, especially if you are using them for good.

I cannot recommend highly enough the practice of good witchcraft. Love magic is especially appropriate and good for you to do. Obeah has answers to the darker side of the craft and, while I promote light, I know there are times when only a negative spell will do.

So do not become a Wiccan if you have a choice. Unless they can prove to me in thought, word, and deed that they're not preempting all of witchcraft as their own territory and worthy of only their belief, then I'm afraid I cannot, in good faith, recommend that anyone believe in their religion. Besides, modern witches work alone, not in groups, and develop their skills in private. That's what makes them sorcerers.

### Superstitions Regarding Babies

The Obeah has a great many superstitions regarding children. A child should never look in a mirror or harm will come to it. A crying child is not to be measured for a coffin. Don't rock an empty cradle or it will bring bad luck to the child. A baby should never be called by its real name, as that will bring bad luck to the new baby—until it is able to comprehend.

The afterbirth must be burned because to not do so will bring bad luck. Also, the afterbirth is sometimes used in witchcraft, and you don't want to leave it around for those purposes.

Look for divination in a small hand-held mirror. You will be able to see the child's future in the mirror at a glance. Cut a child's hair too early and spoil the child's speech. It's like cutting off the child's tongue and powers of articulation. Never cut a child's hair until the child is at least two-and-a-half years old. He or she will talk indistinctly and as one who is tongue-tied if his or her hair is cut too early.

A child is thriving when he or she sneezes, especially when teething. Don't use anything but rainwater when you baptize the child, as the virtue is in the water and makes the baptism more sanctified. The water should be blessed first, of course.

Don't scare a child with the boogy man because a child with an active imagination will become frightened of people.

### *Country Superstitions*

Here is a collection of beliefs held by the African slaves who were brought to South Carolina. They are more superstitions and beliefs than they are magical spells, but they are good beliefs that you should know about.

The slight chilling shudder that suddenly runs over the body is attributable to the fact that a graveyard rabbit is laying out the measure while leaping over one's grave. This superstition is so common that the slight shiver spasm is not called a shiver or a chill, but a rabbit. "It is only a rabbit jumping over my grave" is the most common answer.

If a cat washes her face with her paw, it is a sign of rain. If she elongates herself, stretching and resting her claws against a wall or tree, there will be a storm. If a stray cat follows you or comes into your house uninvited, it is a sign of good fortune to follow. If a cat suddenly fluffs and flies from the room when it is sleeping in front of the fire, she's been stepped on by a spirit warming itself at the fire.

Shovel ashes from the fireplace after dark, and you bring death into the house. Sweep dirt out of the door after dark, and you sweep the love out of the house. Spill milk, and the goats go dry. A howling dog is a sign of misfortune or death. Counter turn your shoes, putting them heel to toe and toe to heel, and the dog will stop howling. Death will be averted.

A scattering of sparks from the chimney and the burning of particles suddenly in the fireplace is a sign of good fortune to come. It means money is coming to the one who is sitting in front of the fire.

To burn eggshells invites sorrow. A rat or mouse that appears suddenly at the chimney corner and that when chased runs across the hearth, betrays the presence of an enemy on an evil mission.

Superstitions that white people believe are very different than those that blacks believe in South Carolina. The number thirteen means nothing to the black man. It's the number three that is evil luck to him.

If your hand has just touched wood and you rub it on a wooden surface then put it instantly in your pocket, it will fetch money. Never brag about good health or immunity from sickness. The spirit of malice will slip in as you speak. If you inadvertently glory in your good health, touch wood at once and rap it sharply three times and the bad luck will recede. Never burn sassafras wood. If it cracks and spits it is the sign of death of someone present. These are all methods of divination and will stand you in good stead if you follow them.

It's bad luck to bury a dog, it pollutes the ground. Plant rice on the spot where the dog is buried. Sow a few rows on Thursday and a few more on Friday night.

If a child is born with his face down or with his hands crossed, he will be a seer of visions, ghosts, or revelations similar to those of a trained guffah man. A baby with these characteristics is said to be born to see trouble, not necessarily to experience woe, but to have a clear perception of trouble and the ghostly forms that go with it. To such a child, dread of the supernatural is unknown. The special child possesses no fear or terror, and the devil shall fear him.

### Reflections in a Mirror

Reflections in a mirror are another powerful force in witchcraft. There are many superstitions surrounding the use of reflections, and one of them is to keep a child away from a mirror. He/she will have trouble teething if he/she sees his/her reflection! He/she will also have bad luck in life if he/she stares at his/her reflection, so keep all babies away from mirrors.

Another source of reflections is the water. It's bad luck to stare at your reflection in the water, so don't do it. Water is deemed to be spiritual, and the reflection in it is demonical in nature, so stay away from watery reflections.

There is an African goddess who looks at her reflection in a mirror. Oxun is her name and she is the second wife of Xango, the fire god. She is very vain and uses her reflection in magic.

I have a friend who is a witch and who lives in Hawaii. She helped me with the Hawaiian spells that appear in this book. I spoke to her recently on the phone, and she shared a spell with me that has to do with reflections. (She found it in a book on Shamanism, but I don't know where it appears so can't give proper credit.) If you write on a piece of paper all your troubles that you want to disappear and put the paper and a mirror in a window, the reflection will take away the troubles. The paper must be reflected in the mirror and then outward to the air. This is a good way of getting rid of problems, and you should concentrate on lifting your burdens as you perform the ceremony of putting the paper and mirror in the window.

### The Subject Is Hair

Hair is one of the most powerful objects in witchcraft. It's connected to you and therefore makes a wonderful connection to a spell about you. Hair has been a subject of attention for men and women over the centuries. A friend of mine as well as Jim's spent a lot of time thinking about his hair or lack of it. I've known Jim for twenty years, and each morning he appears at dawn with a towel wrapped around his head to set his hair in place for the day. He's very sensitive about this, so I hope he doesn't kill me that I've revealed his secret hairstyling system!

In the early 1960s, hair was teased, and to do this you needed hairspray. So I sprayed my hair every morning religiously and then teased it. The result was it began to fall out. I've never regained the thick, ebullient hair I had when I worked at *Glamour* magazine before I started spraying and teasing. But I still have very long hair as Jim, like many men, likes long hair.

Hair should be carefully combed and coddled, especially in public places. Always clean up your hair when it falls in the sink or on the floor, as you never know who wants to harm you with witchcraft. Many spells require the use of hair, and the most potent spell I do requires hair to perform.

There's an old South Carolinian Obeah belief that you should never comb your hair near a window or where there is a breeze. If a bird gets hold of your hair and weaves it into his nest, you will suffer from migraine headaches. Since you don't want that, it behooves you to take care when caring for your hair.

### Guffah Magic

Guffah powers are gifts of the forces of nature, not demonic by any means. Twitching of the nostrils is guffah.

It is lucky if a horse drips saliva on one's garments. No witch will ride your horse if a cow's horn is nailed upon the gable. A watch charm or amulet made of horse hair taken from a living horse, from the blacksmith's shop, is a charm against black magic and Obeah.

To overlook the evil eye of a cross-eyed girl, spin swiftly around and throw rice on the ground, taking steps in the spinning like a high-wire dancer. Spit in your hat and go on. Her evil eye will have no effect.

For a married girl to break a piece of glass or pottery in the kitchen of her new house is bad luck, especially while preparing the first meal there for her husband. A stoneware crock will break the spell if it has a blue border painted on it. It should be rubbed, as there is virtue in the border. Guffah magic is the safest course for avoiding ill happenings.

An old African remedy for arthritis is a cock quill filled with gunpowder or mercury. When worn under a band about one's leg just below the knee garter line, it will take away the pain.

Let not the sunlight fall on your fire as the sunlight doesn't like to be outdone by fire and will take away its virtue.

A black nurse in Charleston will always carry a child head first, never backward, as she wants the child to advance in life, not be backward.

Lusting after women is the same as adultery. You need to go to conjuring to take away the sin.

Sassafras root softens the heart of a woman, as do sweet calamus and sweet flag. To trade spit with your mistress will prevent her from doing witchcraft on you. The virtue of the trade is a mutual preventative against malicious charms. Anoint the stomach with musk oil to attract women. Dry cantharides ground to powder and put into food or drink is a love filter to beget love.

Marijuana also is used in love filters and is made into cigarettes; they produce daydreams. Cocaine takes away the moral fiber.

To cure infatuation, slip a strong cathartic into the drink that you and the woman will take together. To cast off a despairing sweetheart, do the same thing. Put the cathartic in a strong drink.

A wishbone as an amulet is good for melancholia and makes for happiness. Place it over the door and you shall have the love of the first man that enters. Love powders slipped into the shoes of a girl according to the waxing side of the moon will procure her affections and desire for you, even though she may hate you. A lock of your sweetheart's hair prevents her from straying. Mount it with a string or a ribbon and she will be compelled to submit herself to rapture at your bidding.

Shoemaker's wax or resin with pins in it will prevent another man from visiting your girl to make love. Put it under the house door or steps. The urine of a little boy when used judiciously will bewitch a man. Eat salt then sleep. Whoever brings you water in your dream to quench your thirst will be your lover.

### Casting Spells

As you can imagine, I receive a lot of letters from readers wondering why their spells don't work. I will attempt, here, to explain carefully the procedure for casting spells.

Here is a typical reader letter:

I received your book as a Christmas present, and I couldn't have been more excited. I began experimenting and performing all of the love spells with no results. I followed the instructions for all of the spells To Catch A Man and all of the spells To Get

Him Back, because we were lovers. To my extreme disappointment, not one of them worked for or against me to even the slightest degree. I'm not implying that you don't know what you're talking about, but that I don't know what I'm doing. I concentrate until I'm completely drained physically and mentally. I'm at my wit's end. I'm becoming especially frantic because I recently learned that he will be moving within a few months. I greatly need your help.

What this lady has done is muster a lot of concentration on the object of her spell, but she has mustered not one whit of emotion. You need to conjure great amounts of emotion to throw at the object of your spell, mentally, before the spell will work.

Here is the drill. First you prepare the ingredients for your spell and get them ready for the ceremony. Then you conjure a picture of the object of your spell in your mind's eye—it must be a very clear picture. A lot of people fail to do this step properly, and the spell won't work without a clear mental picture of the person you're bewitching. Then you conjure your emotion. If it's a love spell, you conjure love. If it's a hate spell, you conjure hate. Now, telepathically, you throw the emotion at the object of your spell in your mind's eye, and at the same time you do your physical ceremony. This, as the reader points out, is a very draining process. You must be prepared to rest for about an hour after you do a spell properly.

The kinds of spells I'm talking about in this book I haven't written about before. I discovered the Hawaiian spells on many visits to Hawaii, where I lived for several years. I know a Kahuna there who teaches me the spells to perform. They're part of the Hawaiian religion, and Hawaiians get very touchy if you try to adapt their spells for Western interpretation. But that's simply ridiculous. Magic is magic and should be available to all who can access and use it.

The Obeah spells are African in origin. Obeah is a powerful magical belief in the Caribbean, the South in this country, and South America as well as Africa. Wherever slaves settled, Obeah followed. I've hesitated in the past to put black magic in my books, but it exists and some situations call for it. I'm a bit older and wiser now and think I can handle the use of some negative spells. I think my readers can, too. As long as you don't use a spell to try to kill somebody who stole your boyfriend, but use black magic only in extreme cases where real evil has been done, then I don't see anything wrong with including such spells in my book.

You will notice, however, I don't go into too much detail on how to cast death spells in this book. I want you all to be good witches and use your magic for good purposes. But I want you to be prepared for life, and life sometimes has downs as well as ups.

# PART II

## LOVE MAGIC

## *To Get a Lover*

THIS SPELL IS FOR THE YOUNG WOMAN whom I met who was the rock singer. She played with a band that had her sister and brother-in-law in it, and they were on the hotel circuit. She is a beautiful girl and was last heard from in Puerto Rico where she kept an apartment.

It seems this girl, whom I'll call Michele, was on the road so much playing in different cities that she had no private life of her own to speak of. The only men she met were those who might drift into the hotels where she played (she was the lead singer) and those she met during the day when she had to spend most of her time sleeping.

Michele wrote to me in desperation because, when she was playing Minneapolis, she met a young man who came to her concerts. He was tall, good-looking, and blond with blue eyes, and they immediately fell in love. They spent all their free time together, and he even moved into her hotel room while she was in town for two weeks to be close to her and not waste a minute. They were rapt lovers, and Michele felt that he was the one she had been looking for.

At the end of two weeks, Michele moved on with her band to Boston. She was distraught because her love was left behind, and she thought about quitting her career to go back to Minneapolis to be with him. But the lure of the road was such that she just couldn't give it up, and she dreamed of hitting the big time in the music world.

So she and her lover called each other on the phone every night. Since he had a job, he couldn't just leave and come join her on the road as a nonplaying entity. So he was stuck in Minneapolis.

After Boston came New York, and she played at the Holiday Inn on West 57th Street. Her lover flew to join her in New York on his vacation and they had another idyllic interlude, spending a week of incredible happiness that went by at light speed.

Finally, Michele got to Washington and wrote me a letter. She told me where she was playing and could I come listen to her and talk to her about her boyfriend.

I said "yes" because I had never had a reader come to my city and ask directly to see me. So one evening, my friend Jim and I drove over to Virginia where she was playing and met with her in her room.

She was very upset and told me her story. She said she'd read my books, but needed guidance on a spell meant to get a lover to come to you. She wanted him to give up his job and just travel with her as her manager, and they'd be happy together forever (or until their passion cooled). He didn't like the idea, however, because their relationship was so new that he didn't think he could risk his career over three weeks of bliss. But Michele knew better because she was lonely on the road and knew how difficult it was to find a lover who was suitable.

So I agreed to help. I gave her the following Hawaiian spell to get a lover. You must burn some sugarcane in a dish (sugarcane can be found in specialty stores) and, while burning the cane and concentrating on the one you're trying to attract, say over the flame:

> *Join the man and the woman,*
> *Oh great Kane and great Ku,*
> *Bring them together,*

[Mention his name] *and* [mention her name]
*And make them one in heaven.*

## *To Entice a Lover*

I have a friend who went on a trip recently to Palm Beach. She's very well-to-do and has friends wherever she goes. She knew a man who had a lot of money and knew she was interested in Palm Beach.

So I told her to find a way into his house, somehow, when she was down there and to get some hair from either his face or his head if she could. I suggested she sneak into his bathroom and check his razors and brushes. She agreed that she thought she could do that and said she'd call me when she had the items.

One night about ten o'clock I received an excited call from Palm Beach. My friend had managed to get into his house and had collected hairs from his comb and his bed sheets. I told her she had been clever to think of the bedsheets, but asked if was she sure no one else had been sleeping in the bed? She was pretty sure, so we decided to proceed under the assumption that the hairs were his.

I told her to get some sugarcane from a shop in Palm Beach or, if possible, fresh cane from a field if she could find it, then call me again. The next day she called to say she'd driven to the countryside and had located some fresh sugarcane—what was she to do with it now?

I said to cut the cane into small pieces, about half an inch thick, and let it dry overnight. Then, the next night, at midnight, she should take the cane and the hairs from his body and put them in a dish. Then she should set them on fire and burn them while doing the following chant over them. I told her this was going to be a powerful spell so she should be sure that this man was the one she wanted.

She assured me he was the right one and that the match would be romantically and financially correct. I wasn't too sure about the love aspects of this relationship, but I decided to let her pursue her dream if that's what she wanted.

The chant to say over the burning sugar cane and hair is as follows:

*Flame of fire,*
*Purify and sanctify this love*
*And bind these lovers together.*
*Make* [mention his name] *love* [mention her name]
*In oneness of being,*
*Forever after,*
*Until the children are all born.*

Then I told her to do the following: Take the powdered hair and cane and put it in a little box. Take the powder back to his house, if you can arrange it, and sprinkle some of it on his bed while chanting the same spell. Say it twice over while doing the sprinkling, and then take some in the bathroom and sprinkle it around in there and say the spell. All the while you are supposed to conjure a picture of the beloved in your mind's eye and cast the emotion of love from your heart at him telepathically. You do all these things at once, and don't let your attention become diverted because the spell can backfire. You might lose him—never to see him again—if you don't do it properly.

My friend is engaged to this fellow, and he's absolutely entranced by her. They plan to be married in a few months, and she has totally gotten her way. But as I warn, be very sure the man or woman you cast the spell on is the right one for you.

### *To Catch a Man*

A friend of mine named Sally was after a man she met at a party. He was a sweet, dear person who wasn't very practical but was very rich. He was also an artist, and in the course of a year had painted three outstanding pictures, but just three of them. So she didn't expect much of this man in terms of his making a living in the traditional sense, but she was enthralled with his personality.

Sally had some mental problems, such as low self-esteem, and George, the man she was enamored of, was an excellent psychologist and was able to help straighten her out. She became very dependent on him as a result of his psychological help (transference, it's called in psychiatric realms) and so she was forced to ask him to stop helping her lest she completely lose her sense of self and become totally lost in his personality.

All of these situations notwithstanding, Sally wanted to marry this man as he was such a loving, kind person. She had been looking for a man with his qualities all of her life and had always run into the rough ones who cheated on her or abused her in different ways. Low self-esteem problems.

So I told Sally I'd help her with a spell if she'd get the appropriate ingredients for it. I told her we'd need some semen and some fingernail parings. I told her she could collect the semen from her own body after they made love, but that the fingernail parings would be a little more difficult. I suggested that she offer to give him a manicure and use fingernail clippers to collect nails, and a Kleenex to collect the parings from under the nails.

She did as she was told and one night had sex with George and went in the bathroom and put some of his semen in a tiny jar. Then, after he had gone to sleep and rested, she woke him with kisses and a manicure set, whereupon she set about collecting the parings.

She came to my house the next day with her items and we set about concocting the potion to catch him. I mixed the semen and the fingernail parings in a small dish and added rosewater and orange blossoms to the concoction. Then I put them in a tea brewed with chamomile and told Sally she was going to have to drink it. (Don't use more than a few drops of rosewater and one orange blossom.) She was horrified at what she had to do, but was game as she really wanted to marry George.

We were doing this spell not a moment too soon, because George showed signs of wanting to cool the affair with Sally. Once he couldn't tinker with her psyche anymore, he felt he didn't have much in common with her and, therefore, didn't need her around. But Sally was too quick for him, and while they had this discussion about breaking up, the spell was already underway.

Say over the tea, as you're drinking it, the following chant:

> Bring the man to the woman,
> O Amakua of the forests and
> the oceans and the skies.
> Bring the man to the woman and bind them together
> as one.
> Catch [mention his name] and give him to
> [mention her name]
> In the holiest of unions.
> Bring the man and the woman together,
> O Spirit of the heavens and the earth and the moon.

Concentrate on a picture in your mind's eye of the person you're bewitching (in this case, George), and send a stream of love from your heart to the mental picture of the person you love. Repeat the spell five times while sipping the tea and concentrating on the mental picture. He should be yours in a matter of a week, and asking you to marry him within a month.

### *Thanksgiving for a Lover*

I have a long-time lover (twenty years together) whom I absolutely adore and am still in love with. We don't spend every waking hour together as I still work, though he's retired. He spends his days making life easy for me by doing the grocery shopping, all the cooking, going to the drugstore and picking up items that I really need, like stockings. He has his friends that he sees every day, and he generally has a good time without over-stressing himself. And I appreciate him with all my being for doing these things that take a load off me.

Our relationship is inspired. I tend to be morose and depressed, and he is the soul of fun. He tells me jokes when I'm in a bad mood, and I laugh and forget what I had been grumpy about. My latest thing is getting up in the morning—I like time to wake up and think about the day before hopping out of bed to do my exercises and take a bath. I abhor too much routine, and the sameness of every day depresses me. So I need this extra time to get used to the idea of going to work. He wakes up very early (around 4:30) and does his morning ablutions just so that he'll be finished and ready to fix me breakfast when I come out of the bathroom with my hair done and clothes on. Can you imagine anyone more angelic?

I'll never be able to repay him for all the lovely things he does for me. Recently we went to a party at a private club I belong to, and it's mostly women that belong and showed up for the party. But he went and sat there and chatted with these people as if it weren't the most boring thing in the world for him that he could be doing. He's just the perfect man for me and I deeply love and appreciate him.

There is a Hawaiian spell that is a prayer of thanksgiving for a lover who is appreciated and adored. I think it's a wonderful idea for the Hawaiians to have been sensitive to the concept, and I repeat the prayer here. It brings good luck to the lover and long life to the relationship.

Take some sugarcane and a used handkerchief from your lover. Burn them together in a dish after cutting the cane into pieces about half an inch thick and letting it dry out overnight. The handkerchief is to capture his bodily fluids, which is known as sympathetic magic. Take a handkerchief that you've used, and burn it together with the one from him and the sugarcane. As you burn the materials together, say the following prayer:

> *Oh great spirits of the heavens and the earth and*
> *skies, bring this couple endless love together and*
> *from the woman, thanksgiving for her man.*
> *They love each other, Amakua, and need your help*
> *in binding them together for evermore.*
> *Keep them whole and intact, and bring them joy and*
> *love and offspring in their union. May they live*
> *in deep love and holy joining forever.*

The spell will, as I said, bring good luck to him and the relationship and add years to its life. It will help keep you in love and attracted to your soulmate.

### For a Wedding

The Hawaiians in ancient times didn't have a ceremony for marriage. What they did was place a spell on the couple that had come together to bear children fruitfully. So the prayers for marriage are child directed.

My older brother lives in Hawaii, and I go out to visit

quite often, which is partly how I came upon the Huna of Hawaii as an appropriate area for study for modern witches. I've been there twice this year gathering information and meeting with Kahunas, and I've come up with a marriage ceremony that you may wish to consider as part of your own ceremony when you marry.

A friend of mine got married this summer and she used the chant for marriage. The ceremony was held in an inn on a lake in New York State and the bridesmaids numbered six, so it was a fairly large wedding. I was asked what color they should wear, so I suggested hues from the rainbow, for which Hawaii is so well known—red at one spectrum and violet at the other. So she chose a rose and violet combination for the flowers and dresses that was positively beautiful.

The ceremony was traditional, and the marriage vows were the same as those said at most weddings. The only difference was that the minister read the Hawaiian wedding ceremony at the bride and groom's request after the vows were taken.

I give the ceremony here. During it, the couple should hold hands, left to left and right to right, and look deep into each other's eyes. They should concentrate on dreams of love and a happy life together and let love from their hearts emanate toward each other. Here is the Hawaiian wedding ceremony:

> *Oh great Kane and great Ku, lords of all you survey, bring together* [mention his name] *and* [mention her name] *in a joining and union that will bear offspring and love. Pele, raise the fires in their hearts and their loins that they may be joined in sanctity. Find them a place in heaven, Oh great Kane and great Ku, where they may lodge themselves and look down*

*on the earth from the height of their happiness.*
*Bless this union, oh Amakua, and join them*
*with spirits of love and faithfulness of heart.*
*Where once was an empty place there is now a*
*full one with happy voices singing together.*
*Now the two of you are joined as one, and the*
*night leaves you for the day to come.*

*Oh great Kane and great Ku, bless this union of*
*these two.*

### To Fight Impotence

My good friend is in her sixties and married to a wonderful man who is in his seventies. They're Italian, and I visited them not long ago in Rome.

She is a woman who is the head of an organization to keep young couples off the pill and having an abortion by using the rhythm method when they have sex. Her organization has the sanction of the Roman Catholic Church, and the Pope himself assists in her organizational efforts. There are pictures of herself with the Pope all over her home.

Her husband was a businessman who is retired and living the country life. They have a villa that requires a good deal of work, and he spends most of his time in the country working on it.

Between them they had eight children. And they were all planned. Now they've got fourteen grandchildren and others on the way.

When I visited my friend in Rome, she took me aside and confided in me. She said that her husband was losing his sexual potency. She said she didn't mind, but it hurt him a great deal.

I pointed out that he was seventy-one, and that it was

not unknown for men his age to lose their sexual prowess. But she insisted that, in her research, she had learned that men can keep their potency until their eighties sometimes. And it's not that rare.

I said we'd need to do a ceremony with him in it to restore his sexuality if that's what they wanted. She said it was, so she called him in the country to come into Rome the next day.

The next evening we gathered in their Roman house, in the bedroom, and I had him lie in the nude on his back with a towel over his private parts.

I had bought juniper berries during the day, and now I pulverized these in a mortar and pestle. I added some fresh sand from the beach that I'd gathered that day too, and added it to the juniper berries. Now I began my Hawaiian chant. As I chanted, I put some of the mixture on his forehead, his left hand, his right hand, his heart area, his belly button, his penis (over the towel), his left foot, and his right foot. I chanted the following ceremony:

> *Oh great Kane, great Ku,*
> *Amakua of the oceans, the heavens*
> *and the earth, come near*
> *and hear my plea.*
> [Mention his name] *wants*
> *his sexual potency back, and*
> *only you can bring forth the*
> *healing spirits to accomplish*
> *this end. Please call*
> *them forth to this spot*
> *and converge on* [mention his name]
> *so that he may be restored*
> *to the full use of his male organ.*
> *In the name of the Great Spirit,*
> *I call on you all to hear me.*

Within a month of this ceremony, he was having occasional sex again with his wife. He wasn't fully restored because he'd been so far gone, but it was impressive enough to earn me a big "thank you."

## *To Get Pregnant*

An acquaintance of mine was married to a wonderful man, and they decided they would have a child together. At first, they just made love in the usual fashion (after she gave up her contraception methods), and they figured without artificial barriers they would get pregnant very soon.

But this did not happen. So they stepped up their lovemaking. Then they went to the doctor and got advice on the time of the month and the day and hour to make love. And they did this to no avail. Because she'd been on the pill, they thought that was the problem and waited a year for the effects to wear off. That wasn't the problem. No pregnancy.

So they started tests to see if she was infertile, then to see if he was infertile. They both tested normal. Just not getting pregnant was the problem.

So they thought about in vitro fertilization, and they tried that with some of her eggs mixed with some of his sperm in a petri dish and then implanted the mixture in her womb. Nothing happened here either. They had also tried fertility drugs and they hadn't worked.

So in a last ditch attempt to get pregnant, they asked me if I knew of a spell that would work for them. I told them that I did, and that I would help them.

We waited until she was fertile again, at her time in the month when the thermometer said she was ready to become impregnated.

Then we went to their bedroom, and I had them make

love while I prepared the ingredients for the spell. I told them it was important that she have an orgasm, as that would help make the sperm ride up into her system and get her pregnant. So they spent a long time making love, as she was one of those women it was hard to make have an orgasm.

Meanwhile I took orange blossoms, rose water, and the petals from hyacinth flowers (I had to find a florist who could produce these for me). Then I mixed the perfume in a crystal dish and waited for the couple to tell me they were finished.

I went in, and while they were still in bed, I sprinkled them with the perfume I'd made, and chanted the following chant:

> Oh great Hina and great Ku,
>     come to this marriage bed
>     and bless this couple with children.
> They have sanctified their love and
>     their union and now await the
>     fruit of their loins.
> Oh Amakua, draw near and bring
>     good spirits to this chamber
>     and bless this union with children.
> Make them bear a child from
>     their lovemaking, and make
>     the child whole and well. Bless
>     this union of great Hina and great Ku.

Within a month they were pregnant as a result of this session. Apparently the spell did the trick psychologically that the other methods never could alone. They were relaxed and happy and the orgasm worked as well as the chant. Hyacinths are a powerful flower and should be grown in your garden for spells.

### For Mother's Milk

One of the problems new mothers sometimes experience is the lack of mother's milk in their breasts. A woman I know who bore a child when she was in her early forties had this problem. She came to me about it.

Apparently, her baby was sucking and sucking on her breasts but little to no milk came out. She had to feed the baby formula to make up for the loss, but she wasn't satisfied with this solution. She felt, as I do, that mother's milk has special properties in it that affect the immune system and other parts of the body in the growth process, which makes it necessary to have. Mother's milk has very important nutrients that make for a healthy baby.

So I told her we would perform a Hawaiian ceremony over her to see if we could increase her milk supply. We found a smooth, flat stone on the beach, and a stone shot with red and green as well. Then we went to her bedroom, and she took off her upper garments. She lay on the bed, and I put the smooth, flat stone on her right breast and the red and green stone on her left. Then we concentrated on mental images of her breasts being filled with mother's milk.

I took rose petals and sprinkled them on her breasts and over her stomach. All the while I chanted: "Increase, mother's milk, increase in supply and quality." Then I was ready to do the Hawaiian chant. I had her put her right hand on her right breast on top of the stone and her left hand on her left breast on top of that stone. And then I began the chant:

> *Oh great Ku and great Hina,*
> *Come here to this woman in this bed*
> *And inhabit the stones on her breasts.*
> *Settle there and warm her breasts with your presence.*

*I pray to you to bring* [mention her name]
*Milk for her child to her breasts.*
*Make them as full as the mountains and valleys of*
     *the island of Maui.*
*Bring her riches from these mountains and valleys*
*And bring the milk to her so that she may feed her*
  *child.*
*Great Hina and great Ku,*
*I pray you to do this for her.*
*She is a good mother and wants to raise strong*
     *children.*
*Watch over her.*
*And care for her*
*And bring her milk for her baby.*

*Amakua, draw near and bring the spirits*
     *of the woods and the fields and the mountains*
     *here,*
*And bring the spirits of the oceans and the skies in*
     *abundance to this place*
*And let them bless* [mention her name] *with*
     *goodness and richness*
*And give her mother's milk to feed her children.*

## To Get Him Back (No. 1)

I just heard from a reader who has a very sad tale to tell about losing a man and wanting him back. That's what most of you write about, incidentally: getting back lost loves.

In this case, my reader is in the Army and is posted overseas. She practices witchcraft (although she's a Southern Baptist), so she's no novice when it comes to magic. She's no novice about relationships either.

She's married to a man in the States. He's much older

than she is and she doesn't love him. It was a marriage of convenience, as she put it.

In the Army, however, she met a wonderful young man who was her dancing partner in a nightclub. They fell in love across the dance floor and started an affair. He was married, too. They carried on and were happy for a few months, but then he got an assignment to return to the States. She practiced witchcraft to get him to stay, but something was not going well with the spells and they didn't work. He was shipped out. She did a reverse spell so that the affair would end, and it did. But she longs for him and now wants a spell to get him back.

This is going to be very difficult to accomplish as she has already done a successful spell to break them up. We'll have to reverse that spell before doing one to get him back.

To reverse the spell, we'll need something he's touched or used. This could include a letter that he wrote if there's nothing else on hand.

Take the object and chant over it: "Break the spell that I put on him, so that I can get him back. Make (speak his name) return to me and seek no other."

While you're chanting the spell, picture him in your mind's eye in as much detail as possible. Throw emotion at the object, a lot of love from your heart. Wait a week and do the spell again. This one takes time to work, so don't be surprised if it doesn't immediately kick in.

Once the spell is broken and you have him back in neutral, you need to put a spell on him to get him back to you if he hasn't already returned under the influence of the first spell.

Take the object again that you have from him and chant the following spell over it:

*Come to me,* [mention his name],
*And be my love*

*(And draw to me*
*For all your needs.*
*Seek me for love and contentment,*
*And let me fulfill you.*

*Amakua, bring good spirits here*
*To bless our union*
*And may it be*
*Forever more.*

Picture him as you're doing the spell and let a stream of love emanate from your heart. Direct the love down your right arm to your hand and into the object that belongs to him. The spell should work right away, but you should do it again if it isn't strong enough the first time you try it.

### To Catch a Boyfriend

Some of my readers, I've discovered, are very young witches who have boyfriend problems. It's for these young witches that I give a spell that can be used in their very special cases.

Melinda is fourteen and is at that age when she's still got baby fat and is starting to have pimples. She is not her prettiest, and when she looks in the mirror and compares herself to the young movie stars she sees in the fashion magazines, she wants to curl up and die.

What we have to do first is provide a spell that will help in the looks department. If I had had such a spell when growing up I would surely have used it because I went through several years of being overweight with pimples and I was not a pretty sight.

Naturally, the boy that Melinda is interested in isn't interested in her, and he made that perfectly clear when she invited him to a dance that the girls were supposed to invite the boys to, and he just laughed at her. Her feelings were really hurt and she wanted to kill him, but instead she decided that a spell to get him to be hers was what she needed. Hence her letter to me and my decision to help her.

Melinda needs to ask her mother to put her on a diet, first of all. Her mother will probably be delighted and will do so willingly. Then she needs to do my spell to make herself more beautiful.

Get some rose petals and orange blossom water. Put the petals in the water and mix them about. Do this in a pan and heat the mixture on the stove a little bit—just until it's lukewarm. Then put it in a dish that has rose petals on the china, and take it into the bathroom.

Stand in front of the mirror (a powerful magical instrument) and let your eyes stare off into space so that the image you see is double in the mirror. Take your right hand and put rose petals and orange water on your left cheek and forehead. Using your left hand, do the same to your right cheek and forehead. While you're doing this, chant the following spell:

> *Great Hina, great Ku, great Kane,*
> *Make me beautiful as the mourning dove's voice,*
> *As the dew on the grass,*
> *As the whitecap on the ocean.*
> *Bring me beauty to stop the morning wind*
> *And catch the eye of my true love.*

Then to catch the boyfriend you want, follow him around until you can get some sand or dirt from his footprint. Take a little in a tissue and scatter it by the front door of your home. As you scatter it, say the following spell:

> *Amakua, O spirits of mine,*
> *Bring* [mention his name] *to my door*

*Where his footprint is.*
*Bring him to me*
*Nevermore to stray.*
*Give him to me*
*In love and attachment.*
*Bring him here, O Amakua,*
*And I will do your bidding.*

## To Keep a Husband

One of the main reasons women write to me for additional spells and help in putting them to work is to keep a husband. I've never known of so many couples that are on the verge of breaking up that need repairs to their relationship. But they do. And so I will help.

One young woman has a husband who has many girlfriends. Many times when she answers the phone there's a girlfriend on the other end. It drives her absolutely berserk. She's toyed with the idea of murder and suicide and has, fortunately, discarded both ideas. She won't consider divorce because she loves him and can't live without him.

When questioned about his activities, he says the other women are just friends and that he isn't interested in them, just in her. But he's out until all hours of the night, drinking at bars and carrying on with these women, so his story cuts no ice.

In most cases, I would say let's get rid of this husband and, indeed, in a similar case I recommended a spell to get rid of him. But this young woman really wants to repair her marriage and needs help in getting rid of the other women in his life.

I must say I'm hesitant about helping someone who has a situation that is so far gone. It can sometimes be beyond the ken of witchcraft to help and be in the hands of God alone. But I said we'd give it a try, and so we will. If you're in a similar relationship, I recommend that you unload the bum, but if you really want to keep him, then here is the way you do it:

Take a pair of his socks, unwashed, and go to your garden (or out in back of your apartment building) at midnight on the night of the full moon. Take a shovel with you and dig a hole somewhere near the back door of your dwelling. If there's asphalt or cement there, go to the nearest point where there's dirt and dig.

Put the socks in the hole and say the following chant over them as you cover them up with dirt. Picture him and throw great love at his mental image as you do this covering-up ceremony.

The chant is:

> *Keep* [say his name] *from straying from me*
> *With the burying of his feet,*
> *O great Pele.*
> *Bring fire to our union,*
> *And keep him in my house with me*
> *Away from all others.*
> *Let me be the one he turns to*
> *And no other.*
> *Bring fire to our lovemaking, Pele,*
> *So that he'll keep me only*
> *In his arms.*
> *Let this be so,*
> *Or let him die.*

### For a Reluctant Lover

Janice is in love with John, and John lives with Janice in her apartment that her parents pay for. She's very rich, but never has any money as she spends it all on John.

John has told Janice that he isn't ready for a commit·

ment and that, while he likes her a lot, he's not in love with her. He is, in fact, using Janice with her consent.

This doesn't mean they don't argue every day about the situation. Janice wants him to love her and commit to her, and John wants space and isn't in love. Every day they argue about the relationship, and some days they don't talk to each other. Then they make up, and all is well for a day. But soon the argument starts all over again.

John, to say the least, is a reluctant lover and Janice, I fear, is a bit of a masochist. Why else would she choose to love someone who doesn't care for her unless she's a masochist? It's probably the mystery of not knowing whether he'll ever change his mind and love her. After all, he's living with her, she figures, and that must mean something. What it could mean, however, is that he's taking advantage of her since she buys him everything and pays his rent. Or rather her parents do, as Janice doesn't work.

This situation is outlined here to show you what witchcraft is up against—an unwilling lover. This is one of the hardest situations to rectify and takes a very experienced witch. If you still want your reluctant lover for keeps, then read on.

The French gypsies have a spell for getting a reluctant lover to commit to you.

Take an egg and go to a crossroads at midnight. Put the egg in the middle of the road (make it a country one, please) and say the following spell over it:

> *Here am I at midnight*
> *At the crossroads of life,*
> *And I pray, O spirits,*
> *That you grant me my wish.*
> *I pray that* [mention his name] *will turn to me*
> *And forsake all other women for me.*

*Let him love me and care for me*
*Though his heart is hard.*
*Let this egg crack to show*
*The intention of the spirits*
*In this matter.*

Now take a pebble from the crossroads, and drop it on the egg. If you miss the egg or it doesn't crack, then your petition is in vain. If it cracks, he'll be yours forevermore.

Bury the cracked egg by the side of the road while visualizing him and saying:

*Evermore*
*To me be,*
*My love, my husband*
*Stay with me.*

### For the Shy Lover

There was a man who fell in love with a coworker who was also secretly in love with him. He was shy and couldn't get up the courage to ask her out, and when they worked together, he concentrated on their mutual job and didn't pay attention to her physically, so she had no idea that he was in love with her.

They went along like this for about two years—she in love with him, he in love with her, and both not showing it. She showed it a bit more than he did, though. Once, when he was at a bus stop in the rain, she came out of the building and suggested they go for a walk and enjoy the rain. But he was too shy and wouldn't go. He demurred and acted gloomy, and she gave up, left him sitting at the bus stop alone, and went for a walk herself.

And then the unthinkable happened. She suffered a heart attack. It was at work, and he wasn't around when it happened. When he heard about it, however, he realized he was deeply in love with her. The pain he felt when he learned of her illness was terrible.

He went to the hospital and to her room. He had brought flowers with him. He said, before he could change his mind, that he loved her, and she said the same to him. They kissed for the first time in the hospital and promised to talk more as soon as she was better.

They didn't get to this point without the aid of witchcraft, however. Before he went the hospital, I intervened and did a spell on him to keep him from being a shy lover. It's a powerful spell, as you can see, and should be used whenever you want someone to make a declaration of love for you.

The following spell for a shy lover is a French spell that I collected on a trip to Paris. I went to Bibliotheque l'Arsenal and found, in French, some spells from the eighteenth century. Since I speak and read French, I was able to bring several spells back with me, which I've used throughout this book.

The one for a shy lover is as follows:

Take a handkerchief from the shy lover. Cut out a heart from red velvet. Put on a piece of parchment, in small writing, both of your names, and glue the heart over the parchment names. Take a violet flower (you may use candied violets for this) and put it and the heart in the handkerchief. Tie it with a bow of pink satin.

Carry it about with you after saying the following chant over it:

> *Shy man* [or woman], *come to me,*
> *My lover be,*
> *Take my hand in yours in wedlock,*
> *Nevermore to depart from me.*

Then picture the person while doing the chant and throw the emotion of love at the image you conjure. Bring

it up straight from your heart and through your fingertips
to the charm.

Wear the charm until the person declares love for you.
You must wear the charm on your person. A woman
should wear it inside her bra and a man inside his shirt
pocket or underpants. It should be close to your body,
however, to work.

As you can see from the story I told here, the charm
works well. It's a little hard to do, but the best things in life
are not free.

### *To Get Her Back (No. 1)*

The passion Josh had for Sandra was incredible. He loved
her with all his might and with all his heart and soul. And
she stamped all over him.

They had been together for three and a half years
and had spent many happy hours together. They had
gone to sports events and dances and bars (where the
trouble lay) and had a generally wonderful time together.
But then Sandra broke up with Josh, for no apparent
reason, in the month of March. It broke his heart, and he
didn't know what to do, but he just suffered in silence
with the pain.

Then on the Fourth of July he called her on the
phone. She was drunk, and they had a fight over nothing
at all. Then Josh arranged to see her, and, after they slept
together, she told him that she had slept with two other
men since she had seen him. The men she had been with
were strangers to her, and she was drunk both times.

Josh was heartbroken again, but he wanted her back.
He said that he loved her more than life itself and that he
didn't trust any other man to take care of her, just himself.
He wanted to be her protector and lover and to watch over

her. She just said that as long as she knew Josh she was using him. He said that wasn't true.

For all the world, I don't know why such a loving guy as Josh wants a no-goodnik like Sandra. But he does. I decided to help him with a French spell to get her back.

He had to arrange to get from Sandra a piece of her clothing—a glove or a handkerchief or a pair of underpants. Just whatever he could get from her.

Then I told him to put a red candle in a bowl and light it. He took the piece of clothing, cut off a small piece from it, and burned it in the candle flame. As he did this he chanted:

> *Come back to me,* [mention her name],
> *Come back to stay,*
> *Nevermore from me to stray.*
> *Stay with me and be my love*
> *Until our marriage day.*
> *Then stay with me forever*
> *And never go away.*

While he burned the cloth in the flame and chanted, he conjured great love out of his heart and sent it down his fingers into the cloth that he was burning. And then he sent the emotion of love toward the mental picture in his mind's eye.

Making this love connection is very important to the spell and is what will make it work. Concentrate on the picture of the lost love, and she will come back.

In the case of Sandra, she returned to Josh. She proved to be too much of an alcoholic for him, however, and he let her go before too much time passed. But it was on his terms, not hers, so his heart wasn't caught in the obsession with her that it had been. He was healed. What more can we ask of a spell?

### *To Get Her Back (No. 2)*

Eugene wrote to me about his problems and I want to help him. I'm going to recommend the following spell to him and hope that it helps with his situation. First, he has not been doing well with the family business this year, and it's flagging. And his father had a heart attack this year, too, and that makes him sad. And he has stomach ulcers that have kicked up. And, first and foremost, he has lost his fiancée.

The reason he lost her is because he yelled at her a lot due to the financial stress he was under. He lived with his fiancée in an apartment, and they paid out a lot of money for an engagement party. Then there was the wedding coming up and another huge party to pay for. And then, as Eugene said, he wanted to give his new bride a house to live in—not just an apartment—so there were a lot of financial pressures on him.

When his fiancée asked him what was wrong, as she could plainly see there was something, he wouldn't answer her with the truth. He was too proud and didn't want to share his financial burden with her. So he blew up at her, and that made her shy away from him. Eventually she broke off the engagement and moved out of the apartment. This broke Eugene's heart.

Eugene really loves his fiancée and wants her back. He did a spell to get back the one you love, and it worked. She is now riding to work with him every day, but their relationship is more friendly than romantic. So he wants another spell that he can use to get her back completely.

What I'm recommending is an Obeah spell for love. It's strong African magic and may be used by either a man or woman to get a lover back. But I recommend it for Eugene as it pertains to his situation more than many other spells.

Get a piece of clothing from the fiancée. If you can manage a bra or something that she wears all the time, so much the better. Maybe she left a scarf in the house or some other item that she wore frequently. Then take chicken feathers, three of them, and powder (face powder will do, or baby powder), and light a white candle in a dish that's big enough to handle the burning of items.

Cut a piece of cloth from the garment, and burn it with the feathers and the powder in the candle. Chant as you burn the items:

> *Come back to me, O my love.*
> *Return to my arms.*
> *Keep me warm at night with your caresses*
> *And bring me joy with your affection.*
> *Return to me,* [mention her name],
> *And never leave me.*

Then visualize her as you do the burning and chanting, and rouse the emotion of love from your heart, sending it to the picture in your mind's eye telepathically. You can imagine the love coming out of your heart and going directly into the picture you conjure of her.

Eugene should have his lover back in a few weeks. If she doesn't respond, he should do the ceremony again. But only do it twice. If she doesn't respond the second time, then she never will.

### To Get Him Back (No. 2)

Jeanne, whom I know from work, has a desperate problem. She has lost her boyfriend and wants to get him back. This is not just any old boyfriend, but her soulmate, and she's very much in love with him.

They were friends for a year and a half before they

started to date. And when they started to date, they fell in love with each other.

Then, one day, about six months into the relationship, they woke up and kissed goodbye for the day as they normally did. And that was the last time she saw him. This was about a month ago, and though she's talked to him on the phone, she hasn't seen him.

His explanation is that he needed space to work out some problems as he had a lot going on in his life. He said he needed to get away from everyone, but that he loved her and he would be back. At first he was gone for a weekend, but the weekend grew into a month and now Jeanne is going crazy without him.

Jeanne believes that a long time ago the gods were so mad at the way human beings were treating each other, that they separated our souls and put half in one person and half in another—male and female. And now we have to wander the earth looking for the other half of our soul. She felt she had found her soul in her boyfriend.

I told Jeanne I'd help her. She needs a spell to get him back. This is a really straightforward spell situation, and an Obeah spell is the kind to use.

Take the lover's hat and put it nearby. Then take his left sock and wear it. Put the two items together and bury them by the back door, and the missing lover will return home.

Before doing the burying, visualize the lover in full detail and sit before a candle made of pink wax. Gaze into the candle while wearing the sock and the hat and do the visualizing. Chant while doing this:

> *Lover man, come home to me,*
> *And nevermore wandering be.*
> *Stay away at your peril;*
> *Come back home so we can marry.*

Then bury the items. Leave them in the ground for one week; he should be back by then. If he isn't, dig them up and do the ceremony again. If he still hasn't returned after another week, then the spell will not work and you must give him up. Sometimes, the will of God is stronger than witchcraft, and you must learn to abide by His will.

Another spell to get him to return is go to a running stream and cast in two acorns over which you've chanted:

> *Great oaks from little acorns grow.*
> *Let our love so grow and run*
> *with this stream*
> *To the heart of God.*

He should return within a week, and if he doesn't, try it again. If he still doesn't return, then you must give him up.

### To Get Him Back (No. 3)

June writes me that she and her husband, Jonathan, are getting a divorce. They've been separated for two and a half years, and the divorce is going to be final in a few weeks. The only problem is that June doesn't want the divorce to go through.

If you think this is an original situation, think again. I can't tell you how many of my readers have the same problem. They're getting divorces and don't want them.

June says she's still in love with her husband and he's in love with her. She's living in a not-so-good section of town and is going to school. Her husband and his parents, with whom he lives, have the two children from their eight-year marriage. June is afraid he'll find somebody else. But I wonder. If he went home to live with mom and dad where his every need is met and he's treated like a king, will he really want to leave home for another try at marriage?

At least that's what June says. She says mom and dad take care of him in every way and that he's probably spoiled. They're both thirty and have been kicking around for some time now, so she probably knows what she's talking about. But this mother and dad thing doesn't faze her. She wants Jonathan—and the kids—back. Living in a bad neighborhood and going to school, both negative things to be doing at thirty, she probably wants her husband back because she's in need of spoiling. She's probably very unhappy about her life as it is. This is understandable, but she should change her life as much as she can rather than get back in a marriage that obviously hasn't worked.

This advice goes for all my other readers who have had marriages and are getting divorced, but are unwilling to let go. You simply must. When you are happy in a marriage, as I am after many years of searching for the right mate, this is all so clear. There's nothing worse than a bad relationship even if you think you are in love with the man. And I've been there, too, in my search for love.

In any case, you can bring a horse to water but you can't make him drink. So for all you with spouses you're still in love with and want back, here is the spell to get them to come home:

Take a door key to your house and do the following chant over it:

> *Key to my house, key to my heart,*
> *Bring him home to me.*
> *Let him be*
> *With me*
> *In my house*
> *For the rest of our lives.*

While you're chanting this spell, think of him in full detail and send waves of love from your heart to the telepathic picture of him. (This spell works for men wanting a wife back, too.)

Then take the key and go to a dirt crossroad. Bury the key in the middle of the crossroad for two nights. Then dig it up and carry it with you wherever you go, but don't use it. He'll return within a month. If it doesn't work, then go through with the divorce and start life over. We live to be so old these days, we have several lifetimes in one, and this may be the clue to start another one while you can.

### To Forget Him and to Get Him

Janet has written me a letter about her love for a young man who is not in love with her. He's in love with someone else, she thinks and he says, but he tells her all his hopes and dreams and carries on in a loving relationship with her. Let me quote from her letter:

> I met Mike in a club and took him home on a bet (with friends). We spent a year together. We played, cried together, lost a baby together and loved together. All this time he felt he was in love with someone else, but told all his dreams to me.
>
> All our friends could see the love between us, but he couldn't or wouldn't. There is another problem, though, as he's in the Marines and is based abroad.
>
> Sometimes I feel I should forget him, but he is always on my mind and I compare everyone to him. Needless to say everyone else falls short.

Janet definitely has a problem on her hands with this young man. She seeks any kind of advice. My advice is to move on. He's abroad and she's not seeing him on a regular basis. She's doing to other men what he did to her: She's in love with someone else while dating guys who may be potential loves. She needs two spells, really, one to forget him and the other to get him, if that's what she wants.

I'll give spells for both kinds of circumstances and let you use the one that suits your situation the best. It may be like Janet's.

### To Forget Him

You need to take two oak leaves, whether performing this spell in the fall or the spring, and take them to a river. While you drop them one by one into the river you should say the following chant:

> *Oak leaf one, take my love with you,*
> *Down the stream and away from here.*
> *Let my love lessen as you float away into the night,*
> *And in one piece give me back my heart.*

Drop the other oak leaf in the water and chant:

> *Oak leaf two, give me forgetfulness*
> *So that I may not think of* [mention his name] *again.*
> *Silence his image from my mind*
> *And let this be the last time I dream of him.*
> *Float away with his image, and give me peace.*

### To Get Him

Take a thimble, a needle, and red thread and put them in a pink silk pouch. Before doing this, use the red thread and needle to sew a heart on a piece of white silk and put yours and your boyfriend's initials inside the heart. Then put the silk heart in the pouch with the needle, thread, and thimble. Say over them:

> *Bring* [mention his name] *to me*
> *And let him love me*
> *Forevermore.*

*May we be entwined*
*As this silk cloth says,*
*And may we never part*
*Like the needle and thread.*

He should be yours within a month. If you decide to do it over because you don't think it took, burn the first heart and make another one.

## *To Bring Back a Lost Love*

Judith is a young woman I work with, and she has a heart-wrenching love problem.

Her boyfriend of eight years has left her. His sister, who was recently married, didn't like Judith because she was previously married and had a child. The sister thought she was used baggage.

So when it was his turn to marry, the boyfriend left Judith rather than marry her. She thinks it was a combination of cold feet and the sister working away on him that got him to give her up.

Judith says she has tried spells to get him back, but she can't do them properly because she's so upset. She wants me to do one for her. She knows he still cares for her because when her name is mentioned around him, he responds strongly to it. He became jealous when he thought there was another man in her life, for example.

So because I know Judith and I know that she really loves her boyfriend, I've agreed to help her. I'm going to do a spell that doesn't require his hair or clothing because she can't get any bits from him. We'll have to make do without the usual main ingredient in any witchcraft spell.

Here's the spell:

Take a piece of tissue with her spit on it and a sprinkling of salt. Light a white candle in the sink, using a candle that comes in a small glass container if you can.

Chant over the ingredients:

*Bring back my love to me.*
*Bring back my* [mention his name] *to me* [or
        mention her name if doing the spell for
        someone else].
*Lost love rekindle the flame*
*As I burn these objects,*
*So bring back the love.*

Then take the tissue with the spit on it and sprinkle it with the pinch of salt. Make a little bag of the tissue with the salt in it.

Then hold the tissue over the flame and let it drop in the sink to burn. While it burns, concentrate on a picture of him (or the lovers if you're doing it for someone else), and send waves of love down your left arm into the tissue from your pointed fingertip. Then send the wave of love up from your heart to your brain's picture of the man (or couple). While concentrating, say the following words:

*Bring back lost love,*
*Bring back the lover that was,*
*And surround this young man and woman with love.*

The young man should return to her within two weeks. He should call right away, however. This spell only works on people you know, so don't try it on a movie star or someone at a distance from you in time.

### To Get Him Back (No. 4)

Broken hearts and lost loves are the meat and potatoes of witchcraft. I have more spells for getting him back than any other kind because that's what you want most.

Monica has an ex with a twist. He loves her one minute

then, in the next, turns on her and pushes her away. And just as he's getting close to her, he backs off. This is how she puts it in her letter to me:

> I am in love with a man who loves me one day and disowns me the next. I've known him for five years and he can't seem to quite figure out what to do with me. I know he cares but he keeps running away. So, naturally, after the first and second time, my trust in him dwindled. And I feel this distrust is what partly led to us breaking up this last time. Yet I feel a special bond with him. I always have. I just want him to stop breaking my heart and to stay by my side.

He's got her in the double bind: nice to her and nasty to her. She's hooked on the emotional condition he's got her in. She doesn't really love him, because without trust there can be no love. She may experience the feeling of love, but it's just a feeling, it's not for him. She's emotionally attracted to him because he's got her in this double bind. It's a well-known psychological condition and can be treated with visits to a psychiatrist.

But Monica wants to get him back, so I must help her. He won't do what she wants, though, and the situation will just continue. So I don't really recommend that Monica do this spell, and I don't really recommend that you do it either if her story sounds familiar.

I got in the double bind one time, and I went to a psychiatrist to get out of it. It took a year of work, but I realized eventually that not only did I not love the person, I actually hated him for treating me that way. I eventually left town, but I didn't leave in love with a ghost.

To get him back, if that's what you really want, do the following:

Take a gray pebble and a white pebble and a black pebble and put them in a sack made of pink cotton. Add some baby powder (several sprinkles) and three pigeon feathers. Tie the cotton with a silk thread in pink, and carry it with you for a month. Chant over the sack as you're making it:

> *Bring back my love to me.*
> *Bring him back and back to me*
> *Do not let him stray from me.*
> *Let him marry me.*
> *My lost love return,*
> *And return to me.*

After carrying it with you for a month, put it under your pillow. By the full moon of the next month, he should be yours.

As I've warned, you must be careful what you wish for, because this spell won't change his behavior, it will only bring him back to you so you can work on him. And if he wants to keep you in a double bind, he's free to do so.

### For Sexual Potency

Everyone comes to me with problems. I can understand it because witchcraft solves a good many of them. One reader wrote me and asked why I was against black magic when I had some in my first book. I've had to think about this a lot. In my second book I recommend only white magic. In this book, I'm recommending a combination of both as I did in my first book. I've come full circle in my personal growth.

In my first book, I thought black magic was okay in certain situations. I was in my twenties when I wrote it. It was in my early forties when I wrote the second spellbook.

I was horrified by the number of readers who wanted to do others in, so I recommended only white witchcraft.

But in my mid-fifties, as I'm writing this, I think people have the right to do others in if it's an extreme situation that calls for it. Not just because your boyfriend doesn't like you any more, but because your baby's been stolen from you or a lot of money has been stolen from you, things like this. So I'm waiting for the influx of letters from all of you who want to do each other in! I hope you won't but, now that I'm older, I think that black magic has its place.

Now to the subject of this spell. A young man of my acquaintance wanted advice on sexual potency. He says that he's thirty and a virgin because while he's not gay and he feels excitement around a woman when he's nude, he can't have an erection that lasts more than a minute or two. He needs help with his sexual potency.

Maybe he needs to be stimulated by a woman to help him get a proper erection. He doesn't say he's tried this method. We had a very delicate conversation indeed, as you can imagine. But in case he's tried this suggestion and needs something stronger, I'm advising a guffah bag from Obeah magic.

The guffah bag should be made of white cloth (cotton or silk), as he's a virgin. It should be tied with white thread at the top. In it should go the following items: bone (you can use any bone here, but a bone from a chicken is best), red cloth and blue cloth squares, pigeon feathers (three of them), ashes from rosemary and black pepper mixed together, a chicken beak, and a wood charm made in the shape of a penis. Put these items in the bag you make of the white cloth and chant over them:

> *Young woman, come to me,*
> *Make me excited be.*

*Give me strong love*
*And make me whole.*
*Make me make love with you*
*Till I grow old.*
*Make my penis proud*
*And make it strong.*

Then carry the guffah bag with you whenever you want sexual potency, like on dates. When saying the chant, think of yourself having sex and doing it well. Send waves of love from your heart to the picture of your making love in your brain.

It turned out with the young man I've been helping that he can't have sex with just anyone. He has to be in love to have sex, so that's been his main problem. He just wanted sex with any girl he fancies, but he's not made that way. His morals guide his sexual potency so this spell was no help to him.

### *Bring Your Lover to You*

Juanita is a young woman who is a true witch. She does spells, and they work. I tell her story so that you can use the spells she used to get her love to do her bidding.

First, she lost him. He told her that he was in love with someone else from his past that he couldn't get over and that he'd have to drop her because he just couldn't keep up the interest. This did not stop Juanita, however. She performed a spell to hear from him. It worked a month to the day after she performed it. Here is the spell she did:

Take a noose and loop it around a chain and put both the noose and the chain over a white candle. Have his picture nearby, and chant over the spell:

*Come back to me, my beloved one.*
*Call me,* [mention his name],

*That I may win your heart again.*
*Call me, or come to me,*
*But be my love again,*
*And do my bidding.*

As I said, he called her a month after she did this spell and they talked for about twenty minutes. Then, nothing happened. This often occurs with spells. You can lead the horse to water but you can't make him drink. He has to be enticed by you to return once the spell works.

But the hallmark of a good witch is that this doesn't stop her. She moves on to another spell. This is what Juanita did to get her boyfriend back again. First she sent him a Christmas card, and this elicited a short phone call wherein she learned they'd be at the same Christmas party. She showed up all decked out and looking gorgeous, but his interest wasn't stirred. He was still in love with this other woman.

So Juanita did a spell to bring her lover to her. Here it is:

Take his picture and set it near a white candle. Burn together pepper, basil, and rosemary and sprinkle the ashes around the picture. While doing this, say the following chant:

*Obeah man, bring me my love.*
*Bring* [mention his name] *to me*
*So that he'll never part from me*
*Without my wishes making it different.*
*Bring me to him and him to me.*
*In a knot of love tie us.*
*Herbs and spices bless this union,*
*And ashes warm my heart for him.*

Now, just wait. Juanita did and he came back to her about six weeks later. He had given up on the other girl that he was in love with and could concentrate on Juanita. She persisted and prevailed. I give her credit for practicing purely effective magic and adding the interesting dimension of putting his picture near her work. I'm using it in my spells in the future, too; it makes them more effective. You should use a photograph, too, when you have one.

### *To Restore Sex Appeal*

Julie has a boyfriend (or *had* a boyfriend) who got tired of the bacon, as she said. He was with her for a couple of years, and, being a young man, his eyes began to stray. Maybe Julie just wasn't so hot in bed. Or maybe her personality bored him. But for some reason this boyfriend lost interest, sexually, in Julie.

A young married couple, Ralph and Sally, went through financial upheavals of such a nature (he lost $200,000 in the stock market) that she lost her sexuality. She became frigid and that turned her husband off. He strayed. Her sex appeal had vanished.

A couple who had been married for ten years began to regard each other platonically as father and daughter or brother and sister. Their relationship developed into a friendly one without sexuality. Since they regarded each other as relatives, they lost their sex appeal to each other.

These and many more stories are the wages of lost sexuality. It's a very touchy subject, one that affects marriages and close relationships all over the world. You would think, for example, that a husband and wife coming to regard each other as brother and sister were unusual. Not so. It is more typical in older married couples than anyone would think. Once you fall out of love with someone, the sexual part of your relationship begins to change. And it can twist in different ways. Being in love is the key to a lively sexual relationship and should be encouraged and nurtured at every turn.

There is a spell to help restore sex appeal to a lost loving situation. This will be especially welcome news in many marriages.

The key to a good sex-appeal spell is to have someone in mind in order to be able to do it. You need to be close to that person—close enough to get a piece of clothing like tennis shorts or sweats that has a lot of body odor attached to it. You want something really smelly.

Then you take the odiferous clothing and chant over it:

> *Bring me sex and bring it to me.*
> *Make me sexy to be with and around.*
> *Make my lover come to me.*
> *Make him fall under my spell and cling only to me.*
> *May this* [mention the piece of clothing's name]
> *from* [mention his name] *bring him sexually*
> *to me.*

Now wear the clothing around for a day (a Saturday or Sunday is best for this activity). Then take the clothing and wrap it in a plastic bag and hang it in your closet.

While doing the chant, visualize your partner. Keep the image strongly in your mind as you send waves of love and sexual feeling toward the image.

Your lover should be yours again within a matter of days. He or she should not be able to resist this spell, especially if you dress sexily and make overtures that are suggestive of sex appeal renewed.

### To Overcome Age Difference

Jeannette wrote to me about her boyfriend and herself and the sad situation she's in. It seems that eight years ago, she met her love, but she was only twelve and he was twenty-two. They weren't lovers then, but they fell in love.

Now it's eight years later and she's twenty and he's thirty. She still lives with her parents and her stepfather is very much against the relationship.

There were years in between then and now when they did not see each other. Her family had moved eighty miles away. Then on his last birthday, she called him, and the relationship was renewed. She drove to see him, and they've been lovers ever since, but all has not been rosy.

Back in 1989 they were lovers too, for about eight months. Then they drifted apart. There was no upheaval, just a general parting of the ways, nothing you could put your finger on. But when she called him on his birthday, they were magically in love again.

The problems they've been facing have to do with their age difference. Even though she's now twenty, he's thirty and that's a considerable difference. I was once in a relationship that had that age difference, and it didn't work; he was just too old for me.

So what's needed is a spell to overcome the obstacles involved in age-difference romances. The following spell can smooth the way:

Make a salad with carrots, onions, radishes, tomatoes, and cucumbers. Put oil and vinegar on it and toss it. Shave under your arms and put the shavings in the salad.

Now say the following spell over it:

> *Food divine,*
> *Food for the gods,*
> *Make my lover mine*
> *Over the years.*
> *Let not our age*
> *Separate us.*
> *Let not distance*

*Separate us.*
*Let us be together*
*Through all time.*
*Let him eat this food*
*And forever be mine.*

Now feed him the salad, after you've concentrated on him and sent waves of love to the image you have of him in your mind. The vegetables will enhance the shavings from your body and bind him to you.

Your May-December romance should blossom without the impediments of bothersome individuals who think you're too young and he's too old. If they do comment, they won't be able to hurt you or do anything to break you up.

## To Get Your Girl Back

A young man is desperately in love with a young girl. Her mother breaks them up because she feels he's from the wrong side of the tracks. He's using witchcraft to try to get her back.

Sound familiar? It happens to lots of us. I once had a boyfriend from the wrong side of the tracks and my mother and father broke us up. Actually, the boy did it himself by landing in jail. He was caught with a weapon in his car not far from my house, and I always wondered if he was coming to do us in. But that ended the story there for me.

But this particular young man who is in love with his rich girlfriend really loves her. He'd even take an oath not to ever cheat on her or anything of the kind if he could. He was also in a car accident where he could have lost his life but walked away from it without a scratch. That happened in the same week that his girlfriend broke up with him.

So God is watching over this young man, and it

behooves me to help him. Also for the sake of young romance I will do so.

Young romance is the very best kind. It isn't puppy love, it's real love, and adults just don't realize the pain that breaking up can bring. It's like asking a husband or wife for a divorce. It isn't funny; and just because someone has no money doesn't mean that he wouldn't be a good mate. I think that in this country, where color and wealth shouldn't mean much in terms of the person you are, that parents could let their daughters date poor men comfortably. Just because they're poor doesn't mean they always will be. Education has something to do with it.

Now to the spell to get the girl. Here's what I recommend:

Get a snippet of her hair, or if you can't do that, get a picture of her. Light a white candle in a dark room and tie the hair with white thread. Put the picture by the candle and concentrate on it. Say the following chant over the hair or the picture:

> *Love of my life,*
> *Come to me.*
> *Don't ever leave me.*
> *Together we'll be.*
> *Let no one come between us,*
> *Neither father nor mother nor sister nor brother.*
> *Let us forever*
> *Be together.*

Now concentrate on the hair or the picture. Send waves of love in the direction of your mental image of her.

After the ceremony is over (and it's done when you're exhausted with concentrating), put the hair in a white box and tie it with a white ribbon and keep it in your bureau drawer. You should carry the picture with you.

Your girl should be yours again in a matter of weeks. Since the influences are strong to make her stay away, you may have to repeat the ceremony. But wait two weeks before doing so. If she comes back right away, so much the better.

### For Those Unlucky in Love

Many of my readers write with tales of woe about lack of luck in love. Here is a story typical of those I hear:

> I had a wonderful boyfriend, and we were very much in love ten years ago. Then he went and got another girl pregnant, and she got him to marry her. She used her wiles on him and I lost him. It devastated me for years. I was not the same person going in and coming out of that relationship.
>
> Since then I met a young man who I fell in love with but who was an "iceman." He was unable to show his feelings and I was never able to figure out if he was in love with me or not. I didn't see him for several years, and then I called him out of the blue. We started to see each other again, but I still couldn't make headway with getting him to show his feelings. I found out that his father had been like that, too, so it ran in the family.
>
> I never told him how I felt about him because I was afraid it would scare him off. So I've had to live with my love unfulfilled all these years. I feel very unlucky in love.

She *is* unlucky in love. Her boyfriends just don't work out. I think she was so devastated early on that she never really recovered enough to find a warm, giving man. She chose an "iceman" to love who would continue to punish her as her first love did. I understand the syndrome, as I went through something similar. You're so devastated that in some ways you never right yourself unless you happen, as I did, to meet a wonderful warm man who loves only you.

Make a guffah bag of a topaz ring, a small silver box, and a small heart-shaped pillow. You may have to make the pillow to get it the right size. Put all the items in a red satin sack that you make, and tie it with a satin ribbon at the top.

Chant over the guffah bag:

> *Unlucky in love,*
> *Leave me alone.*
> *Bring love my way;*
> *Keep bad luck at bay.*
> *Bring me the love of my life,*
> *And cut bad luck with a knife,*
> *To keep it away from me.*

If you have someone in mind while making the guffah bag, so much the better. You can visualize him while you're sewing the heart pillow and the sack. Wear the sack around your waist under your clothes for a week. Then put it in your drawer with your underwear. Your luck should change almost immediately.

Another spell goes as follows:

Take a topaz ring and put it over a yellow taper. Let the taper burn down to the ring and chant over it:

> *Color of daffodils,*
> *Color of true love and the sun,*
> *Stone of caring,*
> *Bring me true love.*
> *Break the spell*
> *Of my lack of luck in love.*

## *To Bring You Together*

Charlie had been praying for the woman of his dreams to come into his life. He had asked God to send her to him with the good and the bad and that he would take what was given him.

He had prayed the night he went to the club. He was standing there at the bandstand when he felt a pair of eyes on him. He turned and there was the most beautiful girl he could imagine staring at him. He staggered back and said out loud, "Oh my God." Then they continued to stare at each other across the room for a while longer.

One of Charlie's friends knew the woman and introduced her to him. They talked the rest of the evening and went to a waffle house until five in the morning, just talking. They fell in love at first sight and were strongly attracted to each other for the weeks that followed.

The only problem was that she had been in an abusive marriage that she was unloading. He had, too, but had been divorced for some years, so they both knew what abusive spouses did. She pulled back from him and told him she didn't know what love meant. She had lost her mother when she was ten, so had never had a role model to tell her the ways of life.

Charlie asked me for my help. Would I bring them together? He knew this was the woman God had picked out for him and was desperately in love and wanted to marry her.

I said I would try, and that the course of true love ne'er ran smooth, but that witchcraft would help.

To bring them together, I recommend a guffah bag of the following objects: a horseshoe, a magnet, and a comb with a sprinkle of powder and a crab claw. Put these in a white silk bag with thread running around the top, also in white. Say over the guffah bag as you're making it:

*Magnet bring us together;*
*Horseshoe bring us luck;*
*Comb make straight the way;*
*Crab claw feed our love;*
*Powder lighten the way.*
*Bring good fortune to our love*
*And make the romance between* [mention her
        name] *and me grow with the days,*
*And grow strong as the trees and the sky.*
*Bring us together in harmony and peace*
*And make our love sing to the Lord.*

Now wear the guffah bag for a month, until the next full moon, and fondle it every day. While making it, picture your true love and send waves of love to your mental image of her. You should have your love with you within a matter of weeks. Abused or not, she will fall for you as much as you've fallen for her.

### To Rekindle the Relationship

Cindy wrote me to say that she and her boyfriend had broken up and it's killing her. Apparently they met in high school and were together all through the years he spent in the Navy. Then he moved to Washington, D.C., and they continued to be close. She's from Dallas and came for a visit. He called the whole thing off right then.

Why he did this, she doesn't say, but she's heartbroken and needs the help of witchcraft to mend the relationship. The problem is that he's in Washington and she's in Dallas and needs a long-distance spell. She can't get nail clippings, she says, or hair, so she needs to be able to use the items that she does have.

These include a toy bear, his Navy tags, and pictures

and letters dating all the way back to high school. I think we can make a nice guffah bag with these.

Since she's not very experienced at witchcraft, she needs to practice before trying the long-distance spell. She should get a friend to call her from a distance and see if she can do that.

The spell to get a friend to call you is:

Take a piece of coal and put it by the telephone. Chant over it:

> *Call me.*
> *Call me* [mention the person's name].
> *Call me within five minutes.*

If it takes a little longer than five minutes to get the call, don't quibble. But if the friend doesn't call at all, then you need to practice witchcraft some more before trying the more complicated spells.

Now to the guffah bag we're going to make. Take the teddy bear (it's a tiny one, thank goodness), the Navy tags, and the letters and put them in a bag you make of white linen. Use cotton thread to sew it, and put a thread around the top to tie it.

Now chant over the items:

> [Mention his name], *come to me,*
> *Nevermore from me to stray.*
> *Take my hand in wedlock, pray.*
> *Together for all time we'll be.*
> *Mine you'll be,*
> *Yours I'll be.*
> *Divine our love will be.*

Now wear the guffah bag for a month until the next full moon. Then take the contents and sleep on them under your pillow for a week. He should be yours before you know it. It'll be a long-distance romance that suddenly becomes close-by. He'll call you and then come and see you.

Most of the letters I receive are from people who have lost loved ones to broken romances. So if there are a lot of spells in this book for this condition, this is why. People need help, and witchcraft provides it.

### To Attract Women

There's a young man who lives in my building with whom I'm pretty good friends. He's a computer nerd, not bad looking, and works for the Justice Department. He's a lawyer, but women aren't very attracted to him because he's not the handsomest guy in the world.

This fellow spends all his time on the Internet, e-mailing messages back and forth to friends he's made on his computer. He just doesn't have any real-life girlfriends to do things with. So while he's not lonely, he would like more human contact.

I've suggested the use of Obeah, as my friend's a hunter and can get the ingredients for the spell he needs to become irresistible to women.

In fact, we went hunting together and caught a fox, which is what he needed for his charm.

Take the intestine of the fox, or a muskrat, and dry it out. Put a small piece of it in a locket and wear it as an amulet. You should also wear a piece on your left arm under your clothes as this is the strongest magic for attracting women.

Chant over the amulet:

> *Bring me sex*
> *Bring me women*

*Bring me adventure,*
*O fox* [or muskrat].

The amulet should start working at once. If you tie the intestine around your left arm, it should work fast. If you put it in a locket, it won't work as fast but will be effective.

### To Get Him Back (No. 5)

Once you've done something to a man, he never forgets it. The same can be said of a woman. So if you've done something to someone and they're angry with you, then you'll have to resort to witchcraft to straighten things out.

Until last month Debbie had had a boyfriend for four years. She's an alcoholic but is in Alcoholics Anonymous. But after a year of not drinking, Debbie picked up the bottle again, and her boyfriend threw her out (understandable enough). She was heartbroken and quickly stopped drinking again, but is tempted to drink again because now she's lost her dear love.

What problems people make for themselves! What a double bind situation! First you lose your boyfriend because you drank, then you want to drink because you lost your boyfriend. It seems unfair, but life is like this. And there are millions of situations that have this double bind effect. You can go right down the tubes in a double bind.

Debbie is really in love with this man, however, and she thinks she's strong enough not to drink. She thinks she may be able to get him back if she doesn't drink, so she's going to try.

Meanwhile, witchcraft can come to the rescue and bring him back to her. If he still loves her, he'll come back. If he doesn't, well, that's another story.

The spell to bring someone back when you've made a

mistake and have made them angry or turned off by what you've done is as follows:

Make a boy doll. Sew little pants and a little shirt (a T-shirt is fine), and put hair on his head. Use some of your own hair to make the doll's hair.

Take a net (a hair net will do) and wrap the boy doll in it. Chant over it:

> *Doll that is the image of* [mention his name],
> *Caught in the net of my love for you,*
> *Come back to me now*
> *And let me embrace you.*
> *Fall for my charms*
> *And let me tie you up in the web of love.*
> *Doll that is the image of* [mention his name],
> *Bring him back to me*
> *That I may love him and marry him.*

Now take the doll in the net and bury it by your front doorstep. If you live in an apartment, tie it over your front door on the inside.

While doing the chant, picture your lover clearly in your mind's eye and send waves of love to the image you project. Send the message out over the miles to your lover, and he'll call you within a short period of time. It could be a day or two, so be patient.

# Part III

## HATE MAGIC

## To Cause Misfortune

I KNEW A WOMAN WHO HAD a son with a promising future as an astronomer. He was attending the university near where I live, and he had everything to live for. Unfortunately, he was one of those young men who felt that he was different from others; so shy, so withdrawn socially, that he turned to alcohol and drugs to assuage his emotions and anxieties.

The drug dealer who got him his stash was a predatory man in his thirties who had an evil heart. He would talk to my friend's son and tell him that he was no good and that he would never amount to anything. After a while, the boy began to believe him as this drug dealer was an older man and knew him well. He knew all his weaknesses and fears and played one against the other as the young man got deeper into drugs.

Eventually, the drugs and alcohol caused a depression so severe that the young man went to a psychiatrist to see what was the matter. He didn't realize the drugs and alcohol were the reason for his depression; he just took them for his psychic pain. But drugs and alcohol are a mortal enemy when in the hands of an addict, and that's what happened here.

The psychiatrist could do no good, and the drug dealer kept telling him what a horrible human being he was. So after a while, the man's will was worn down and his depression grew so great that he decided to end it all.

The mother, meanwhile, saw what has happening to her son and talked to him about what the drug dealer told him. She said that it wasn't true that he was evil and that he needed new friends and help from a counselor on drug addiction. But this advice did no good, as addicts don't listen to advice that's going to separate them from their drug supply. So one night the young man went to the roof of the building I live in (which is an eight-story building) and he jumped off.

The mother was distraught and told me about her anger with the drug dealer. She told me that this man had just as good as pushed her son off the roof because that very evening he had told her son what a useless human being he was.

I gave the mother a spell to work to cause misfortune to the drug dealer. I told her she had to concentrate on his face when she chanted the spell, and that she had to throw huge emotion at him telepathically. I also told her to be careful to do this in a darkened room alone, while concentrating on a candle flame, and to make certain there were no sources of distractions nearby, such as the telephone. I told her distractions could cause the spell to backfire on her, and if she wavered in her concentration on the drug dealer's face the spell could backfire.

She was adamant about trying it, however, and she knew her cause was just which is the only occasion on which you should ever cast a spell to harm someone. Here is the spell:

> *Oh spirit of the heavens and the earth and seas,*
> *hear my plea.*
> [Say the name] *has been wronged and spat upon by*
> [say the enemy's name] *and needs restitution.*

*Bring the powers of your winds and fire and water*
    *to bear on* [say the enemy's name] *so that he*
    *will fail and grow weak.*
*Make* [say your friend's name] *strong and prevail*
    *in this battle.*
*O Kane of the heavens and mountains,*
*Heal the wounds of* [say friend's name]
*And bring power to bear*

*So that* [he/she] *may have* [his/her]
    *way with* [say the enemy's name].
*Bring Mana here and correct the error.*

## To Get Rid of a Love

A friend of mine had a boyfriend for five years that she
needed to unload. He had an alcohol problem, and when
he drank every day (he didn't work as he was too far gone),
he cavorted with other women and often slept around.
This would enrage my friend, who was supporting him
because he couldn't work due to his alcohol problem, and
this carrying on with other women took place while she
was at work.

This fellow was the type to hang out at the betting
parlor and the shoeshine shop as well as the bars in the
neighborhood. When she called him at the shoeshine
shop one time, she heard him scream in the background:
"Didn't I tell you never to interrupt me while I'm fuck-
ing?" This was yelled at the shoeshine shop owner.

My friend went into a tailspin at that point and, having
a drinking problem herself, increased her intake of alcohol dramatically. I told her that she had to break off this
relationship as it was going nowhere and could eventually
be dangerous—he had threatened her several times.

I really worried when he bought a gun. It seemed that

the only person he was going to use it on was her. So I took it upon myself to call the police and tell them he was carrying a gun and, when they checked, he was taken to jail. It was illegal to carry guns in that state.

I told my friend that she had to do a spell as soon as possible to get rid of him. She finally agreed, even though she was psychologically tied to him and eventually had to see a psychiatrist to break the hold he had on her. So one evening, after another drinking and fighting episode wherein he pushed her and she fell over the coffee table and broke two ribs, she came to me and said she was ready for a spell.

We took some hair out of his comb and brush and burned them in a small dish while chanting the following spell:

> *Break the union of* [mention her name] *and*
>     [mention his name].
> *Utterly destroy the bond between them*
> *And make them whole again,*
> *Alone and in peace.*
> *Break the union, O Kane, O Ku,*
> *And come Amakua to this place.*
> *Take away the spirits that caused them to join.*
> *Break the union, O Heavens.*

Then we took the burned hair and sprinkled it in the four corners of her apartment and put a few ashes on their bed.

While chanting the spell, I had her concentrate on a mental image of her boyfriend and summon as much negative emotional thought about him as possible. It came out a little as disdain, but it was an overall feeling of good riddance. I had her direct that emotion to the mental image she conjured of her boyfriend and had her cast the emotion into the dish with the burning hair as she chanted the spell. She said the spell three times, and then we did the sprinkling of the ash.

In about a month, the boyfriend was completely out of my friend's life. He came home one day, packed his belongings and cleared out, not even telling her where he was going. This is a powerful spell when properly done, so you should be pretty certain you want someone out of your life before attempting it.

### To Get Rid of a Lover

Jocelyn has a boyfriend she wants to get rid of. He's violent, and he threatens her when he's drunk. She told me the following story:

She was at home studying, as she's going to school for economics, when her boyfriend came home from the bars around 1 A.M. She was sitting on the couch when he walked in, and he was very drunk. He told her that she was the reason he was drinking and that he was very angry that she had this power over him. He said that he was going to kill her to get rid of her influence.

My friend had a gun by her side. She picked it up and pointed it at her boyfriend. He lunged for her and the gun went off. He was hit in the stomach and fell to the floor bleeding. She called 911, and the police and ambulance came.

She told the police her story, and the hospital confirmed her boyfriend's blood alcohol level. He began to heal and decided not to press charges. She was arrested for having a gun, however, but it was decided that she had fired in self-defense.

I was horrified by this story and told Jocelyn that she would be a fool to go back to her boyfriend, as he was begging her to do. She agreed with me, but was in love with him and was in a psychological double bind. She needed him, hated him, and loved him, all at the same time. This is a common occurrence in violent relationships. The only way to get out of them most of the time is through counseling.

So I told Jocelyn I'd help her with a spell to get rid of her violent boyfriend. Here's what I suggested:

Over a pile of his possessions that he uses all the time, such as his comb and brush, toothbrush, shaving cream, razor, and aftershave lotion, do a little ceremony. Burn a picture of him over a dish in front of the pile of his most personal possessions. Concentrate on his face and body as you burn the picture, and summon great revulsion as you do the burning. Say the following chant which originated in Hawaii:

> *Hina, Ku, and Kane, come here and help me to rid*
> *my house of* [mention his name].
> *He is violent and no good for me and needs to leave*
> *right now.*
> *Amakua, come here and rid my home of evil spirits*
> *brought here by* [mention his name].
> *Cleanse the premises and bring good mana here to*
> *free me of this man.*
> *Great Hina, Ku, and Kane, I pray to you and to the*
> *oceans, land, and air that you represent and to*
> *your spirit of healing.*
> *Bring health back to my house and get rid of this*
> *man for me.*
> *Empty my house of him as I empty my house of his*
> *image.*

### To Get Rid of the Other Woman

One of my good friends lives in Hawaii. She's a very free spirit and believes that aliens are here from the Pleiades to help the human race. She's also studying to be a Kahuna and practices what I call witchcraft at an advanced level.

My friend is fifty and has a boyfriend in his late twenties. She says there is no sex and that they're basically just good friends, but I find that hard to believe as she's so beautiful. Anyhow, she's in love with this young man and was distraught when he started going out with another woman.

My friend is an artist, and her boyfriend helps her with some of her artistic pieces, so it's very important that they not break up as her livelihood depends on the relationship.

He's a quiet young man with an earring in his ear and long hair. But I know he loves my friend —he's just young and doesn't want to get involved exclusively with an older woman.

But that doesn't matter to my friend. She's in love and needs him around for her work. She sometimes talks of letting him go, but I know that in her heart she doesn't want to. So it came as no surprise when she told me she'd put a spell on him so that he'd drop the other woman.

I asked her if she'd share the spell with me, and she said she would. I doubt she thought it would wind up in this book, but I haven't used her name so I'm sure it's okay.

She found out who this other woman was and where she lived. Then she posed as a salesperson and got into her apartment. While the girl had her back turned or was out of the room for a moment, my friend took a used tissue from the pocket of the girl's coat.

My friend then returned to her house and burned the tissue in a bowl while chanting over it:

[Mention her name] *leave* [mention his name]
*alone and don't go near him again.*

*Stay away from my lover and keep your eyes to*
    *yourself where he's concerned.*
*Burn, body fluid, and stay away from* [mention his
    name].
*Stay away or I will harm you and send Amakua*
    *after you to torture you.*
*Stay away from* [mention his name], *as he belongs*
    *to me.*

Take the burned tissue and, in front of a mirror, scatter the ashes in the bedroom. While burning the tissue, concentrate on her face and throw powerful angry emotions at her image. You must discover, if you're going to do black magic, where the darker emotions reside in your body. To summon them you must know what you're doing, as dark spells can easily backfire.

As I said, my friend is an experienced witch and knows what she's doing. Be careful if you try this spell as it may harm you if done incorrectly.

### The Other Woman

This spell is for the woman who is being wronged by another woman. I wish it weren't so, but the competition for men goes on apace. This story is currently going on, so it's very sensitive.

Annabelle has lived with Roger for fifteen years. He's a psychiatrist who is retiring soon, and Annabelle works for the World Bank. They have a mutual friend, a woman, who is also a psychiatrist, and they've known her for about as long as they've been together.

The female psychiatrist's husband has recently left her for a younger woman. Naturally, she's distraught and in a great deal of pain (or so she says). Roger is a very attractive man, and this female is calling on him to support her night and day. Roger is acting as her psychiatrist and mentor, and Annabelle is beginning to become jealous.

Another mutual friend and I think the female psychiatrist is after Roger since she's taking up all of his time and Annabelle is being left alone in the evenings. My friend says, beware of the man who wipes away the widow's tears as she will soon have him as a lover. Annabelle has been told this by my friend, and now she's really jealous.

I know Annabelle and Roger well, and I'm very upset for them that this woman is coming between them. It could break up a (formerly) perfectly wonderful relationship and put an end to the sparkling parties that Roger and Annabelle throw every now and then. I will mourn their passing, as the parties are catered and very elegant.

I really care for the two of them (all party jokes aside) and want to help. So I've gone to Annabelle with an offer of assistance. I've told her I'll do a spell to get this other woman out of her life. All Annabelle is doing, currently, is arguing with Roger about the situation, and that's going to make him turn away from her even more.

So I've asked Annabelle to have the woman over for dinner one night so she can collect hair from her head. Annabelle can do this by offering to fix a "stray hair" that she will say she sees on the psychiatrist, and then she can pull it out and have the thrill of pulling her hair at the same time as getting some to use for witchcraft.

I'll have Annabelle urinate and put the urine in a little jar. Then I will put the woman's hair in the jar with the urine and say the following spell:

> *Hair and urine mix and mate*
> *Rid me of this woman and don't be late.*
> [Mention her name] *wants my husband in her arms.*
> *If she tries again, bring her harm.*

While holding the jar and chanting the spell, concentrate on the victim's face and throw strong emotion at the image. If you can muster hate, do so. I really don't recommend doing this spell yourself without the help of an adept witch as it can backfire. Every time hate is involved there is a chance of disaster. I felt sorry for my friend, so I chanted the spell and drew the emotion for her. But then, I'm an experienced witch. I rarely do spells that involve hate, however, as I only believe in love. But my friend was in desperate straits, so I helped her this once.

## Two-Timing Woman

My beloved Jim, with whom I've lived for twenty years, goes to Starbucks Coffee Shop every morning for a cup of brew and conversation with the regulars who come in.

One of the men with whom he talks every day is a fellow with a terrible romance problem. He's become involved with a two-timing woman. She's young and has another boyfriend besides this man. She told Jim's friend that she was going to give up the other fellow, but they had an argument and she trotted him out again.

This time, she told Jim's friend that she was going on a trip with this guy to think things over. Jim's friend couldn't do a thing about it, so when they went on the trip, he haunted them night and day with phone calls. This upset the girl so much that she and the other man returned early from their vacation.

She was very angry with Jim's friend for interfering, and in a moment of weakness, this man said he'd pay for a trip for her to Mexico so that she could think over her choice on the beach by herself.

This is where I came in. The girl was in Mexico and I learned of the man's predicament. I told Jim to tell him to get me something that she wears quite often and that I'd put an end to her two-timing ways.

I didn't hear from Jim's friend for some time, and then one day Jim showed up with a dirty pair of stockings. He said they belonged to the girl and that Jim's friend wanted a spell put on her as she had taken up with the boyfriend again.

So I took the pantyhose and said a spell over them:

> *Woman of fire, woman of steel,*
> *Woman who is nothing but a heel,*
> *Turn back to* [mention his name]
> *And turn back quick*
> *Or you will soon*
> *Be in a fix.*

Then I took the pantyhose and, with a shovel, buried them in the backyard of my apartment building. This spell is double trouble, as the pantyhose are far away from their owner and in a strange spot. So she'll never be able to get the spell back or taken off her as she doesn't know where the stockings are.

As I buried them, I did a French spell over the site of the burial:

> *Two-timing woman may you never return to your*
>     *lover,* [mention his name].
> *Feet, walk to the tune of* [mention his name] *and*
>     *never more stray.*
> *Or may death come your way.*

This two-part spell should have the effect of her giving up the boyfriend and staying with Jim's friend only. That's what he wanted and that's what he'll get.

### For the Other Woman

There's a girl I know who has had nothing but big trouble this year. She was engaged to a man she was very much in love with, and she thought he was in love with her. But it turned out that this wasn't the case.

She had a best friend who was going to be her bridesmaid in the wedding. Much to her chagrin and broken heart she discovered that the best friend and the fiancé were having an affair.

What's worse, the best friend still wanted to be friends with her and tried to apologize for having the affair with the fiancé. This woman's actions cut my friend to the quick, and she just couldn't wait to get rid of her and her evil ways.

The woman who was my friend's best friend cried and cried and was very sorry for what she had done. My friend sat there listening, stone faced, but didn't say a word. Then she asked: "What do you want me to say to you?" And the best friend said: "I want you to be my friend again." And my friend said to her: "What do you mean by friendship? What's your definition?" And with this her best friend cried and cried. Then she said: "A person to confide in and be there for you." And my friend just hurrumphed and laughed at her former best friend. What could this woman have been thinking of? She made love with her best friend's fiancé and then wanted the wronged woman's friendship back.

So my friend said she needed a spell to deal with this woman and her peculiar ways.

I said I would help. So I looked through my African Obeah spells and came upon a good one for the other woman. Here it is:

Write the other woman's name on a piece of paper and stick a needle, not a pin, in it. Drop the paper and needle in a bottle and put a candle in the top of the bottle. While lighting the candle, picture the rival in full glory and in great detail. Throw enormous disgust at her image (hatred, if you can muster it), and then let the candle burn all night, right down to the last drippings. Then take the bottle and bury it near the house of the other woman. It should be as close to her doorstep as possible.

If you can't muster hatred, disgust will do. For a God-fearing person, it's very hard to conjure hatred and it's not a good thing to do in the first place. But Other Woman situations often call for strong measures, and sometimes hatred is the only emotion that will do.

When dealing with hatred, you have to practice to see from what point in your body it comes. It may come from the stomach or the area of the pubis. Or even from behind the eyes. You need to know from where your emotions are conjured to get the full effect of them. So experiment until you're sure you know the seat of your feelings. Your body is an instrument, and the emotions play across it all the time. Many of them are seated in the stomach, and love, of course, comes from the heart. Love is the easiest to conjure and the most powerful of the emotions; it's even stronger than hatred. Good witches need to know all of their emotions so that they can help others.

### To Cause to Wander

My friend Beth had a terrible problem that only the most dire kind of punishment seemed to remedy. Her husband was unfaithful.

Beth was in love with her husband, John, who was a lawyer, and the two of them had three very beautiful children. They were all young and at an age when to be fatherless would have been almost unthinkable. But John was a faithless husband in the worst way, and Beth couldn't put up with him any more.

She showed up at his office one evening when John said that he was working late. She had a key to his office suite and walked in to find him naked and having sex with another man. She had married a bisexual and didn't know it.

Beth said she screamed and the other man pulled on his pants as fast as he could. She would have committed murder right there if she could have, she said.

But I had something better than murder in mind for Beth. I have a spell that will cause a person to wander the rest of his life, once it's properly done.

Get dust from his footprints, dust from his clothes, and white pepper from a shaker. Take them to a flowing stream and throw them in while chanting:

> *Nevermore come home,*
> *Wander through your life,*
> *Always be alone,*
> *Lost and filled with strife.*

The person will have a life of trouble thereafter. You'll be entirely rid of him or her.

## To Part Lovers

I know a young woman who has a situation with a man that she thought she wanted so she did a spell on him. She's an experienced witch in that she's done several major spells that have worked, including this one, so I didn't hesitate to give her an Obeah spell that's very powerful and takes experience to work.

She met her young man through a dating service. She had just broken up with her boyfriend of five years and had been off the market so long she had no contacts for getting back in the dating game. So she went to a dating service for help and put personal ads in the newspapers.

The dating service came through for her with a young man who, while he wasn't very good looking, had a lot in common with her. They both loved computers and tennis and walks in the woods and travel. So they spent week-nights on the Internet, weekends playing tennis and going for walks in the country, and vacations traveling to exotic places. They were very happy together, and my friend put a spell on him so that he'd marry her.

Then he started to weird out on her, and she dis-covered that one of the Internet people they'd been talking to had been meeting him for lunch and they had fallen for each other. He was carrying on an affair behind her back. This was much too much for my friend, so she decided to get rid of him. She came to me for help. I gave her the following spell to part lovers. She didn't want him back, but she wanted to part the new lovers.

I said that she needed to get pictures of the woman she was trying to separate from her lover. She needed nine of them. So my friend followed her boyfriend to one of his trysts and took a camera with her. When they met, she started snapping away. They had gone to a restaurant, so it was pretty easy to catch them in the parking lot without being seen.

Then I told her to do the following: Take three needles and break them into three pieces each (use a wirecutter for this). Write the lovers' names on nine slips of paper and wrap the pictures and the papers together, each with a piece of the needle, sand from the street, and red pepper.

Take the papers and pictures to the woman's door and bury them there for nine days. You can't use this spell at an apartment building as it's too disperse there—unless there's a doormat at the woman's apartment door, then you could put the pictures under her doormat.

Then on the ninth day, dig up the papers, take them to a running stream, and throw them in. One of the lovers will forsake the other.

I will add to the Obeah spell to make it work even better and more specifically. While making up the nine packets, picture the woman in your head and throw emotions of revulsion at her image. The emotion comes out of the stomach and jaws and should be mustered strongly as you're doing the spell.

The woman's lover broke up with her within two weeks of her doing the spell and left the other woman, too. He moved out of town to follow a new job. The Holy Ghost must have been listening in to this spell, as this is the kind of mysterious way in which He works.

### *To Do In an Enemy*

You need a really good reason to use the following spell. It's a deadly Obeah spell and leaves the victim in a total state of disarray. It brings disaster to the object of the spell.

One such case that the spell has been used on that I'm aware of is the situation with Janelle. She's a very rich woman and a close personal friend of mine. With money, which is what is involved here, it's not how rich you are but the principle of the thing that counts.

Janelle knows June, a girl who lives in Washington in a house on Fourth Street. June didn't always live there; however, her mother did, and it's around the mother this story revolves.

June's mother grew sick and became hopelessly ill with

cancer. She hung on for only a few months because the lung cancer had gotten into her body organs. By the time the cancer was discovered, it was too late to do anything about it.

So June's mother died, and June went to Janelle and told her she didn't have enough money to bury her mother. Could Janelle loan her three thousand dollars that would be repaid when she inherited her mother's money? So Janelle gave her the money for the funeral. The only problem was that June took the three thousand dollars and went to Europe and didn't spend it on her mother's funeral at all.

Janelle was horrified by this betrayal and knew she'd seen the last of her three thousand dollars. She asked me to help her with a spell to cause harm to June for the betrayal, and I agreed to help. The following is the powerful Obeah spell that we put on June:

First you need a bit of paper or cloth belonging to the victim of your spell. You can get this by any ruse that could masquerade as a favor. Like you could volunteer to take the victim's dress to the dry cleaners or have the victim write a letter of some kind that you intercept.

Anyway, get the cloth or paper and smear it with human filth. This is the disgusting part (wait, there are others) and should be done discreetly in your bathroom. Then put the paper or cloth with the filth on it up the colon of a chicken. It can be a store-bought chicken. If you really want to be authentic it should be a turkey buzzard, so if you live in the country, by all means get one of these.

Then take the chicken or the turkey buzzard to the home of the victim and hide it somewhere about the place. Then when the moon is high, urinate on the victim's doorstep.

Once this is done, the only way to keep disaster from

striking the victim is to use lye to clean the steps, or urine from the victim himself or herself, followed by a leaching with salt.

The spell should work almost immediately, and the doing of it should be accompanied by a lot of disgust and hatred emotions brought to bear on the image of the victim of the spell.

The disaster can take any form, so look out for anything untoward that happens to the victim. It's a powerful Obeah hate spell, and if you're lifting it, don't forget to retrieve the turkey buzzard or chicken from the house of the victim.

### For a Faithless Husband

One of my readers, I'll call her Janice, has a terrible story to tell, and it's ongoing. She's in need of a spell to bring her good luck, as well as a fetish against the man she married.

She married a foreign man; his nationality isn't important. They were married for three years and were very happy together, with lots of dreams and material goods. He told her that his father died when he was young and his mother raised him, and that his sister had died of cancer some years ago.

Well, all was well and going along smoothly until last Christmas when we went back to visit his mother and the children his sister left with her on her death. He told my reader he planned to bring them back with him to the United States so that they could have the good life, too. Janice agreed to this plan, as they didn't have children and she thought she could look after the little ones. His mother was getting old and needed to retire from their upbringing.

Then he left for his trip and wrote her saying that he

had lied to her and that the children were his and he was married to a woman who wanted him back. He wrote that his sister and father were fine, and that he wouldn't be returning to the United States.

My reader was in a state of shock. She not only was in shock but in very real trouble as her money soon began to run out. Sh-2e worked for $5.50 an hour, and her salary didn't begin to cover car payments (it was repossessed) or the mortgage. She was on the verge of losing her house when she wrote me in desperation for a spell. Here are the spells to help her.

The good luck spell I had for her was a French spell and goes as follows:

Take a piece of parchment and write your name on it and the words "God Bless My House And Keep It." Do this in fancy script, or have someone you know who knows how to write fancy script do it. Use blue ink on white parchment.

Then roll the parchment and tie it with a blue satin ribbon. Sleep on it for six nights and on the seventh, a Sunday, burn the parchment in a candle flame. The candle should be blue. Scatter the parchment ash, when it's cool, around the premises while chanting "God, bless my house and keep it." This will bring good luck and help you keep your home if you're on the verge of losing it. The money to pay for it should come to you through a second job or some other means.

Now to the fetish for the husband. This is an Obeah spell and should be done with malice toward the husband who was so faithless and evil. Get the skull of a small rodent, the wings of a butterfly, buzzard wing feathers, an embryo chicken in an eggshell, and the dried intestines of birds or animals. Wrap these in a black cloth and tie with black string. Say over the fetish:

*Evil to him*
*Who evil did me.*
*Bring him down*
*And crush him for me.*

Then carry the fetish for ten days and bury it in a graveyard near a new gravesite at night. Evil should befall the victim in a matter of a few weeks.

### To Get Even for an Evil Deed

I heard about the following story through a friend of mine and decided to help when I realized what a terrible situation it was.

A young man had an alcoholic and drug addict as a best friend. He kicked both habits and, since they had been school friends, the good guy was willing to help his best friend when asked. And he was. The best friend asked for the good guy's credit card so that he could buy his wife a washing machine. The good guy thought about it, realized his friend was off drugs and alcohol, and decided to let him have it.

Instead of returning the credit card after buying the machine, the evil friend kept the card and charged six thousand dollars worth of goods on it. The good guy was horrified, but the evil guy said he would pay him back a little at a time as soon as he got a job. He had lost his when he was drinking and drugging. So the good guy got his card back and could do nothing but pay off the evil guy's bills.

This proved to be impossible, however, as he just didn't have that kind of money. He went into bankruptcy and the creditors were after him over these bills. Eventually his marriage began to fail, and his wife left him. They had been arguing over the stupidity of the good guy for letting anyone have his credit card, even though it was his best friend whom he's known since grade school.

The evil guy had terrible conscience attacks, but not enough to get a job and start paying his friend back. He told everyone that he felt bad about the trouble he'd caused, but couldn't do a thing about it.

The good guy thought he *could* do something about it but just wasn't trying to do anything. And that's where I stepped in.

I told the good guy I'd help him, but that there wasn't anything we could do to get the evil guy to get him his money. What we could do was make a negative fetish and bury it near his house to bring him enough bad luck so he'd have to get help and come out of his drug-induced funk. You guessed it; the evil guy had really never gone off drugs and alcohol. He had just gone underground with it.

So we concocted an Obeah fetish consisting of chicken feathers, gunpowder, skeletons of rats, squirrel parts, cocks' bills, crab shell, and gall. (Gall is the part of the body of an animal that has the most black magic in it, and after it's used in the fetish it should be burned separately and the ash scattered to undo its bad luck.)

We put these ingredients in a black silk bag that I made with a black silk ribbon to tie the top. Then I said the following chant over the fetish:

> *Bad luck bring to* [mention his name],
> *He's caused evil.*
> *Evil come to him*
> *As he did to another.*

Then take the fetish and bury it near the back door of the person to whom you're doing magic. This should bring him down a notch or two very quickly.

In the evil guy's case, he lost his house and he and his wife became homeless. Only after being homeless for the winter months did he seek help for his addictions. Now he's really coming into his own and is much better since he has a program to belong to. He should be able to start paying my friend back sometime soon.

### To Get Even With Him

I know of a woman who has a most terrible situation. She is a woman of forty-six, and her husband, who is fifty-nine, has kicked her out of his marriage bed. He says that he doesn't love her, that he hasn't in years, and he's taken a young lover, a woman of thirty, to replace her. He's filed for divorce and has taken up with this girlfriend.

The woman who has been wronged has tried a number of spells from my love magic book to get him back. But that isn't really what the situation calls for. She has been wronged and needs to get even with him.

This woman, Shelby, says she isn't a witch and that's why she's having such trouble doing my spells. It may very well be the case. She isn't very competent right now anyway, and that may be a problem. Since she's not an evil woman, I can't ask her to do a spell against him to get even with him. But I can help her along.

The husband is a very handsome doctor, according to Shelby. He is used to having his own way and is a very selfish man. He really had some nerve to kick Shelby out of the house and tell her she was no longer wanted or needed. I can't imagine how terrible she felt about this situation. She wants her husband back, but I don't see any hope for that. I think her best bet is to punish him and let it go at that.

I think an Obeah charm is the best magic in this case,

something we can bury by his back door. He's changed the locks so whatever Shelby has of his is all we can get, unless she could arrange to get into the house and get a dirty pair of underpants. That's what I'm going to need for my spell on him.

I'm making a fetish bag of black silk tied with a black silk ribbon. In it I'm putting the crotch from his dirty underpants, a red clay devil's head that I own, an alligator's tooth, chicken droppings, dog droppings, road dust, dried tadpoles, red cloth torn from a garment belonging to a convict, and a tissue with the excrescence of pimples on it. I do the following chant over the bag:

> *Guffah bag, guffah jack, do your work at the home*
> *of* [mention his name].
> *Bring unhappiness here, and the evil eye,*
> *And break up the girlfriend that* [mention his
> name] *has taken.*
> *Get even for the sake of his wife,*
> *Who has been wronged.*
> *And if he does not regret his deed,*
> *Pay with his life.*

Then take the guffah bag and bury it near his back door. Within two weeks the couple should break up. After they have, take the ingredients out of the bag and cleanse them with a prayer ceremony to take off the evil influence. (To do a prayer ceremony, say over the ingredients the Twenty-Third Psalm, and your ingredients will be cleansed and ready to use again.) The droppings you can just throw away.

In the case of Shelby, her husband and girlfriend broke up in a week and haven't talked since. Shelby tells me that she is trying to get her husband back as she thinks this woman bewitched him and he was under her power. That may well be the case, but I merely broke up the bad relationship. The rest is up to Shelby.

## *To Get Even*

They say that all is fair in love and war and some people literally believe this is true. Of course it isn't because if you do bad things to people, you might just go to hell. So you must very selectively choose the situations in which you need to do black magic.

Here is one of those circumstances that requires some of the black arts. I heard about this one through a friend of mine and was horrified by it. I recommended a black spell to the person it happened to through my friend, and I don't know if it was used. But I'll share it here with you.

This man and woman were happily married and enjoying life together. But there was a woman who was jealous of their relationship and wanted to break them up. So she told the husband that the wife was cheating on him, and she told the wife the husband was cheating on her. Naturally both mates told each other it wasn't true, but the seed of doubt had been planted.

It wasn't long before the wife started to question her husband's whereabouts if he got home late from work or had to go out to do volunteer work on the weekends. And the husband wondered about his wife's boss, with whom this evil woman had said she was cheating, and would watch to see if his wife was at all disheveled at the end of the day.

Eventually they broke up. Their mistrust in each other was too much for the marriage to take. The evil woman who broke them up then made a play for both the wife and the husband, as she was bisexual, and was roundly rebuffed by both. But the damage had been done, and the marriage was beyond repair.

The kind of spell you need in a situation such as I've described is a strong Obeah spell. You need to be ruthless in how you go about getting the ingredients for this spell. You need some hair from the victim's head, and you need an article of clothing or, at the very least, a used hand-kerchief or tissue.

The way you get these is to invite the victim to your house for a chat and put your arm around the victim and pull her hair. Then you excuse yourself and go in another room and preserve the resulting hairs. You get a tissue by offering one to the victim and then taking it away once it's been used. You could arrange to put something peppery near the victim so she will sneeze and need a tissue.

Once you have these items you take them to the bathroom and pee on them. While doing this you chant the following:

> *Liquids from me curse this woman*
> *Whose hair and hanky these be.*
> *Bring her ill health and trouble*
> *And make her life a misery*
> *For hurting me.*

Then take the hair and tissue and wrap them in toilet paper and put them someplace safe. After they've dried out, burn them in a black candle's flame and scatter the ash in a running stream while doing the chant again.

The woman should have no peace and her health should deteriorate. That's what she gets for breaking up a perfectly fine marriage.

## To Dump Him

Samantha has a problem that only the police can solve. She wrote me a letter about her situation, and I agreed to help her because she's so desperate.

Samantha met Abe in April, and they hit it off at once. They lived in Hawaii and spent time on the beach and in downtown Honolulu in the shops and bars.

He said he worked for a living, but he seldom went to any office though once in a while he took trips for his company. She thought he was an undercover cop from what he said and the care with which he got himself around. Anyway, the mystery intrigued her and she was hooked by him.

They fell deeply in love and spent all their time together when he wasn't working. He worked at odd hours, like the early evenings and late mornings, but nothing alarmed Samantha about this.

The only arguments they had were when he took these out of the island trips that he sometimes did. She wanted to go along, but he wouldn't let her. He said he'd be gone for a few days and that was that.

Then when one such trip came along, he told her that they were finished when she argued with him again. He said he was tired of arguing about the same things over and over and that there was no future for their relationship. But as soon as he was back in Honolulu, he called her. This was a good thing, she thought, because she found she was pregnant.

He was ecstatic about the baby coming and spent even more time with her. Their troubles seemed to be over, until the next time he had to take a trip.

Then he admitted to her he was a drug dealer and that he was getting supplies when he was off island.

Samantha knew immediately that she had to ditch him. Just arguing with him didn't work, now, because of the baby and his desire to be a father. So she wrote me for a spell. I sent her the following one to do, as she's an experienced witch and can do advanced spells. You shouldn't try this unless you're advanced, too.

Get some feces from the victim. You can do this by offering to share the toilet after he's unloaded before he flushes it. Put a piece of the feces, a pork bone, a dead housefly, and a dead cockroach in a guffah bag of black cotton with a black cotton thread at the top. Chant over it:

> *Leave me instantly.*
> *Leave me alone.*
> *Never more come near me.*
> *Let me be free.*

Then burn the guffah bag with a black candle and throw the ash in running water (the ocean, in Samantha's case).

The spell to get rid of him should work very quickly. Whenever you have the victim's feces, you have something that is the most personal belonging that you can have from them. Concentrate on ridding yourself of him while saying the chant, don't forget. The spell is a potent one so be sure you have a good reason to dump him in this fashion.

### To Punish Him and Get Him Back

Crystal has a problem that many of my readers have. And she wrote me about it and asked for my help.

Crystal had been engaged to a handsome young man for about three months when he told her he was going back to his former girlfriend. He said he was still in love with this woman and wanted to marry her.

This wiped out Crystal. She tried to commit suicide, but was found in time before the pills had taken their full effect and was hospitalized for several weeks. She received psychiatric care in the hospital and is now, she says, receiving counseling. Attempting suicide was a terrible thing for her to have done, but it's understandable given the amount of emotional pain she was in upon losing her fiancé so suddenly and in such a fashion.

Crystal can't let go, however. She wants him back. She's still in love with him, she thinks—though the emotion may feel like love, it probably isn't. They still talk to one another on the phone. They had agreed that if anything happened in their relationship and they broke up, they'd remain friends. To even think of this concept, I'm sure that all was not well from the beginning and that something dire was afoot.

But it's my contention that to just get him back won't do the trick. He needs to be punished first. He needs to be humbled before Crystal should take him back. Anyway, she wants him back so here goes.

### To Punish Him

Take his picture and three needles purchased from a voodoo shop. Ask around, you can get the address of a shop in New Orleans that sells them, but you need the real thing. Place the needles in the picture of him where you want him to hurt. Then chant as you're doing this:

> *Needles of fire, needles of pain,*
> *Bring punishment to* [mention his name].
> *He's wronged me to no end and needs to feel the*
>     *pain of what he did to me.*
> *Make him feel pain where I put these needles.*
> *Let him suffer as I have.*

Then twist the needles in the picture as you're inserting them. Concentrate on his face and body and send waves of hatred to the telepathic image you've created.

### To Get Him Back

Remove the needles from the picture after three days

and put them away until the next time you need them (should you need to repeat the spell on a recalcitrant lover). Then take the picture, or another one, and sprinkle it with rose water. Chant as you're doing this:

> *Come back to me my love,*
> *Be mine forevermore.*
> *No more from me to stray*
> *But marry me now.*

Picture him and send waves of love toward his image. If you can do this, you must still love him and deserve him back.

### To Fight a Tormentor

Susie is a friend of mine who has a fourteen-year-old daughter. She's going to be fifteen soon and has a fifty-three-year-old boyfriend. This came about when the daughter was walking to school one day and passed a house with some men working on the roof. One of them was singing a song that the daughter liked and she called up to him. He came down from the roof and they started to talk. She asked him for some gum and he didn't have any, but the next day he brought her some.

Their relationship was started, and Susie is being tormented by this man. Her young daughter has been taken away from her and has moved into this man's house. She plans to marry him in April, and Susie is fit to be tied.

This man has ruined Susie's and her daughter's lives by insisting that he carry on a relationship with so young a girl. Susie needs a spell to fight the tormentor. He brings gifts home to this young girl every night and takes care of all her needs. Susie has visions of them sleeping together, and it's killing her. The daughter, as you can see, is headstrong and won't be controlled by her mother. She just laughs in her face when Susie tells her to come home and live in her house again.

Susie has asked me for a spell to get rid of the man who is tormenting her so. I've provided her with such a spell; it can be used on anyone who is tormenting you, no matter the circumstance.

Take three hairs from a horse's tail and tie them together with red ribbon. Cut them so they're even on both sides of the ribbon. Chant over the hairs:

> *Hairs from the horse,*
> *First animal of God,*
> *Take away* [mention his name]
> *From my house and my kin.*
> *Keep him from me and mine.*
> *Run away with him,*
> *And keep his evil ways*
> *From me and mine.*

Now take the hairs that you've chanted over and visualized the tormentor as you've done the chant, and tie them to the house of the tormentor. If he lives in an apartment building, tie them to his apartment door. Leave them there for three days then take them down and find a swiftly running stream. Throw them in while chanting:

> *Carry away the evil that is* [mention his name]
> *And his evil ways.*
> *Take them far away,*
> *O fleet horse and stream,*
> *And let them nevermore*
> *Come my way again.*

You should be rid of your tormentor within two weeks. He won't bother you again; and in Susie's case, she got her daughter back.

### *For a Cheating Man*

Here's another situation that required magic to punish someone. This one comes from a reader, Mary, who wrote me the following letter:

> We have had our share of the everyday arguments that all couples have. I think it was my fault that we broke up, and I may have made a mistake in judgment. I accused him of being with another girl. He wasn't very happy at all with that. He broke up with me and said I was possessive, that nothing ever happened at all and he and the girl were only friends. Well that wasn't true at all. Eventually the truth came out. He said it happened once and it happened the night of our big fight and that it was a mistake and didn't mean anything. There have been others. He says he never meant to hurt me but that this is just the way he is. He wants to be able to see other people and not have the responsibility of a relationship.

Mary has her hands full. I'll give her credit for being like the FBI and tracking down her cheating man. Most men who cheat get away with this kind of nonsense.

There's nothing for a case like this but to punish the guilty party. Of course, Mary wants him back, but I'm not going to help her get someone back who is so untrustworthy. He would just continue to hurt her, even though witchcraft could return him to her. She can use one of my other spells to get him back, but a cheater should be punished, especially if you have the means at your fingertips. Incidentally, Mary was engaged to this man, so he wasn't just a passing fancy.

What Mary must do is get an article of clothing from her fiancé. Maybe she can invite him over and sleep with him and steal his underpants, but she needs a really personal item of clothing to do this Obeah spell.

It's always a good idea when you're involved with a man to steal some item of clothing to use against him if it should become necessary. This goes for a woman, too, if you're a man. There's nothing so potent as a bra. So acquire the article of clothing when the going is easy. Also, get some hair. It's always good to have hair on hand.

Now take the underpants and wrap two rocks in them, good-sized rocks. Now chant over the underpants:

> *Clothes of* [mention his name], *blaspheme his name,*
> *Write his misdeed against the sky.*
> *May he never have a moment's peace,*
> *So long as these rocks are in his clothes.*

Now take the underpants outside and bury them under a tree in your back yard. Speak to the tree:

> *Guard these clothes, O tree,*
> *And grow around the rocks*
> *To make him squirm.*

Your lover should have no peace for days on end, and the spell should bring him all kinds of small misfortunes.

### To Get Rid of a Rival

I'm the resident witch at work, dispensing spells to my co-workers at their will. I've just came across another situation that needs my help.

Jodi has a friend who is in a relationship with a young man of whom she's very fond. In fact, she wants it to work, but the guy's ex-girlfriend keeps calling him up at the house and it's putting a strain on Jodi's friend's relationship. It wouldn't be so bad, but the two of them are currently living together and the ex-girlfriend is certainly making life miserable for my friend's friend.

There are several ways of handling this situation. The best way is to get a photograph of the girl and take it outside and bury it under a tree. The girl will go away soon using this method. But if you don't have a picture, what do you do?

You can blow a whistle in the phone and hurt her eardrums when she calls. That's another method not using witchcraft; very effective, however.

You can light a candle and throw a handful of the herb rue into it, and chant:

> *Get away from* [mention his name]
> *You unwanted woman.*
> *Leave him alone*
> *And leave me alone.*
> *Leave our happy home*
> *And don't come here anymore.*

While you chant the spell, you must concentrate on an image of the offending woman and cast hatred at her. You have to have a very hard heart to do this spell.

But the most effective spell for getting rid of a rival is the following Obeah spell:

Make a guffah bag of three black feathers, a sprinkle of baby powder, a length of telephone cord, and a watch. Put these items in a black sack with a black satin ribbon around the top. Say the following chant over the guffah bag as you make it:

> *Woman, leave my man alone.*
> *Leave my happy home alone.*
> *Don't come near me,*
> *Or you'll die.*

*Don't come near my man,*
*Or you'll hear him lie.*
*He'll turn you away at my request,*
*And you'll nevermore be heard from.*

Now concentrate on this other woman as you make the guffah bag. Bury it near her house or apartment building under a tree. Leave it there until she stops calling your house. She *will* stop calling, too, as this is a very powerful charm that you've made. Wear an amethyst ring while trying to rid yourself of the other woman; it will bring you good luck and hurry the process along of making her go away.

### To Punish

I was written to by a woman who's beside herself with anger. She's been in love with a man for three years who not only cheated on her but threw her away for another woman. She's so angry she wants to do him in, but I think we should punish him instead.

Carol says in her letter to me: "I bought groceries for him, bought fuel oil so he wasn't cold, and tried to help him make ends meet. I bought expensive gifts on special occasions and I did his laundry for two years, besides everything else." She is really humiliated.

Apparently, she was going to move in with him and was bringing some things to his house when she walked in on him with another woman. She wanted the floor to open up and swallow her, she was so undone.

So what did the cad do? He moved in with this other woman. She's living in the house with him now, and there's nothing Carol can do about it short of murder. That's no good, so witchcraft will have to do.

Carol says that all she's got from him is some pictures, a pair of socks, and a toothbrush. That should do it, especially the socks.

The trouble is that Carol has been doing some spells from my other books and nothing has happened. So she needs something not too complex that's effective. We're going to do a Witch's Ladder on them and put him in the hospital.

Take the pair of socks and sew them together with red thread. Just one stitch will do, and leave a long thread because we're going to tie knots in the thread—five of them, about two inches apart.

While tying the knots in the thread, chant the following:

> *As I tie these knots,*
> *May your stomach knot.*
> *May your heart beat faster,*
> *May your liver give out.*
> *As I tie these knots,*
> *Let your health go bad.*
> *Let your teeth rot.*
> *Let your life be sad.*
> *As I tie these knots,*
> *Let your life fall apart,*
> *And let these knots be your undoing.*

Now concentrate on him as you tie the knots and chant the chant. Memorize it so you can concentrate on speaking with hatred projected at him with ESP and at the picture in your head. Only the highest degree of hatred will do, so practice the emotion before doing the spell.

Hatred is a tricky emotion to deal with because if you don't get it just right, it can backfire on you. You might wind up in the hospital, so it's nothing to fool around with, and you must be pretty certain you want to do the hate spell before you try it. It should start working right away. He might injure himself, or be in a car accident or something pretty quickly.

# Part IV

## MAGIC FOR ALL OCCASIONS

## Treating the Sick

I HAD GREAT SUCCESS when treating a sick friend with a prayer from the Hawaiian Huna. My friend went to Paris with me, and we had the most incredibly wonderful time. We saw friends of hers, took the Bateau Mouche around the Isle de la Cite, and went to the Musee d'Orsay. We had lunch at the Ritz Hotel and visited Chanel, and I went to my favorite occult library (Biblioteque l'Arsenal) where I handled a seventeenth-century manuscript on witchcraft. We ate at the most fabulous of the French restaurants that are newest and choicest. In short, we had a really wonderful time for a week. But through it all, my friend suffered from a severe illness.

She had what seemed to be asthma, and it caused her a great deal of misery. She almost missed the Bateau Mouche as it was too far for her to walk from the pont to the actual launch site. When I was comfortably on board, I heard her trill. She had found a cab to take her from the bridge to the boat and made it just in time. But the asthma controlled her, and her breathing was labored and difficult.

So I, one convenient evening, lay her upon her bed and sprinkled the bed with orange blossom water to purify it. I let some of the droplets fall on her, and as I did the purification, I said the Lord's Prayer.

After my prayer, I envisioned my friend as well and whole and without the asthma. I kept the image of a relaxed and well woman in my mind and I said the following Hawaiian chant over her:

> O Amakua of the ocean, the land, and the skies,
> Heal [mention the person's name] from the
>     illness that inhabits her.
> Amakua, swarm around her, [say the person's
>     name], and heal [say the person's name],
> And complete the healing.

I repeated the prayer three times, sprinkling rose water on my friend as I said it. She was nude and was relaxed almost to the point of sleep.

After the ceremony, she went to sleep for the night, and in the morning the asthma seemed to have released its grip a bit. She was able to sit up at breakfast and have coffee without gasping for air and was able to walk, using her cane, to the Louvre for lunch in the Pyramid.

What occurred after we got home from Paris was astonishing and tragic. My friend went to the doctor to see why the asthma had gotten so bad (she thought it was the air pollution in Paris that irritated her lungs).

The diagnosis was lung cancer. But the good news was that the tumor hadn't spread and was just locally growing in her left lung. It may well be that the Hawaiian ceremony helped to contain it, as it definitely blossomed on our trip.

My friend is undergoing a course of chemotherapy and my prayers are with her night and day. This is the first time that a friend of mine has been seriously ill, and it's a terrible shock to withstand. She may well have her tumor reduced when she has radiation therapy and live another fifteen years. We all pray for her, and I plan to do the ceremony again at her home midway through the course of her chemotherapy. It may strengthen the effect and will certainly give her hope. It's very important to keep a good attitude when very ill.

## A Guardian Spirit

An Amakua is a guardian spirit that comes in the form of a bird or a small animal of some kind. The Amakua is sought for its good luck and help in times of crisis and generally watches over the individual who has one. It's found by calling on one's ancestors to seek and find the spirit that is one's personal protector. Since it's a very good idea to have a nature spirit as a guardian, I've enclosed here the prayers for getting one.

You need to make an offering, and an appropriate one would be a glass of wine and a bowl of fruit. Place them on a table arranged as an altar, and say the prayers over the offering while picturing a deceased family member who can help you find an Amakua.

For a male Amakua, suitable for anyone to have, say the following prayer:

> *Heavens and spirit*
> *Of the earth and seas and skies,*
> *Listen, O spirit,*
> *Bring Amakua from the rainbow,*
> *From the sun and sacred lands.*
> *I bring you an offering.*

At this point, the petitioner makes his offerings, calling the god's attention to each one. He then prays as follows:

> *O great Kane,*
> *I sing to Kane,*
> *I talk to Kane,*

*Kane of the skies*
*And oceans and lands.*

*I beg for an Amakua*
*To come to rest here,*
*To come inhabit this space*
*In time and spirit.*

*To Pele,*
*Goddess of fire and volcanoes,*
*I sing your praises.*

*To Kiluea,*
*And the many spirits*
*Of fire and water and air,*
*Come close here and now*
*And bring your powers to me.*

*I seek an Amakua*
*To protect and guide me,*
*In all my days,*
*In my coming and going.*
*Brush aside the darkness,*
*Brush aside death,*
*And come into this world of the living.*
*Give me power.*

Try to learn the chant a little bit before undertaking the ceremony. You may read the prayer, however, and the pronunciations are pretty much as the words indicate. Modern-day Hawaiians who trace their roots to the way of the old culture all have an Amakua, so you should have one too. Call on one when you want something or when a crisis transpires in your life. An Amakua can help you with your desires.

### To Protect From Evil

There's a woman I know who was having an affair with another woman's husband. She didn't realize that he was married because he lied to her and told her that he wasn't married and that, in fact, they would someday be married themselves.

My friend believed this man, and the relationship stretched on for five years. Then, one day, upon close questioning, he told her the truth. He said he was still married and that his wife was an extremely jealous woman.

Immediately, my friend began to suspect that the wife had cursed her because everything in her business life had gone wrong in the past five years. She had lost a job for one thing, and then the next job she got was at a much lower level than she should have been. She just never recovered her station in life although she sent out hundreds of résumés and networked at the appropriate organizations where she would meet people in her chosen profession.

Curses are very real in today's society. There are so many people from all over the world who settle in the United States and they bring with them the traditions of other cultures. Nine times out of ten when the culture is third world, magic is a part of the tradition. There are many experts wandering around our streets on how to cast curses.

I told my friend we'd have to find an adept who could test for a curse to see if one had been cast on her. We did find one, a Brazilian woman, who knew the Obeah well, and she tested her. It turned out she had been cursed, and I set about organizing a ceremony from the Hawaiian Huna to remove it.

Sometimes if the curse isn't professionally done, it's

enough to say: "What you have given me, go, return to (say the sender's name)." Or you can say, "Go back and destroy your keeper." Thus the malevolent spirit that is causing the curse can be removed and returned to the person who ordered it against you. But sometimes the spell is stronger, and a prayer is needed to remove it.

Kill, dress, and cook a white rooster. When it is ready, feed the person with the curse some of the meat. Tell the spirit that it is for its nourishment and that it should be grateful. The spirit should then make an inquiry: "What do I do to repay your kindness?" You say: "Go to your keeper, the one who has sent you here. There find your home, your food, your drink, your mats. Destroy your keeper and that will be your gift to me." Then you need to say a chant over the accursed:

> *O Kane, remove the curse*
> *That is here in the bones of* [say your friend's name],
> *And great Ku, bring your power to bear*
> *And hear our plea.*
>
> *We pray for this curse placed by* [say the enemy's name] *to be lifted,*
> *And order restored to the life of* [say your friend's name].
> *Bring peace and harmony back to* [say your friend's name],
> *And lay the curse at the door of* [say the enemy's name].
>
> *Amakua, guard the soul of* [say your friend's name]
> *And keep it pure from the curse that is there on it.*
>
> *Send the curse back full force,*
> *And double its power on the sender.*

*Make this curse powerful enough to shake the*
     *heavens and the earth.*
*The skies should quiver in dismay.*
*Bring the power back to* [say your friend's name]
*And let* [him/her] *prevail in this battle.*

### *For Protection*

As an author on witchcraft, I am often subjected to the black arts by people who are angry at me for one reason or another (for example, they tried a spell I recommended and it didn't work). I received a letter from a reader who practices Wicca and some black witchcraft, too, I fear, and this person was really huffy. Out of ignorance, this person didn't realize I was describing classical sorcery, but thought that I had made the books up.

I was very annoyed but didn't respond to the reader. I can't as a rule respond to readers, as most of my advice is in my books, and anyway, when readers write, they're venting. It could have been that this Wiccan was venting, too, but I found that I became worried about the anger I'd felt in the letter and decided I needed to find a protective spell to guard me against random acts of witchcraft.

At the same time I was casting about for the appropriate chant or spell for protection, a friend told me that she had her artwork in a gallery where a woman, who was a bit on the spooky side, began to ask her for money that she didn't have for a loan. My friend's close friend told her to get her artwork out of the gallery as soon as she could because she knew the woman practiced the black arts and might try something against her if she didn't come up with the loan.

So my friend, who lives in Hawaii, decided to do some research for us both to find a protective spell, and after searching the bookstores and consulting a Kahuna friend of hers, she found one that works wonders. If you have need of a protective spell because someone is doing witchcraft against you, the next spell will help you.

For my reader who wrote and said that her mother was trying to put a spell on her because the mother wanted her daughter's boyfriend, this is the spell for you. I can't imagine a mother being so hard up as to want her daughter's boyfriend, but this girl swears that it's the case and the boyfriend even wrote to me and said the mother had tried to seduce him.

In any case, if you have a situation where you need protection from witchcraft or from the evil eye that someone may have given you, here is the way the Hawaiian Kahunas recommend that you protect yourself:

With this spell, you are calling on the multitude of gods that the Hawaiians have to protect them, and you do this by lighting a candle and chanting the following over the flame. Try to keep the person's face in your mind who put the spell on you if you know who it is, and summon as much emotion as you can while chanting:

*O great Kane and Ku,*
*Come near and listen*
*To our plea to you.*

[Say the person's name] *needs protection*
*From curses and chants of an evil kind,*
*And calls on you to protect* [him/her] *from such evil.*

*O Amakua of the forests and skies and seas,*
*Draw near and lend your power of protection*
*Against curses and spells of all kinds.*
*Bring your influence here and circle around*
    [mention the person's name]
*To protect* [him/her] *from evil and the work of bad*
    *spirits.*

## *Prayer for Illness*

There's a woman at my work who has been very ill with cancer. She got it, I think, because she's a very cold person without much emotion and is very distant to those around her. I don't think it's because she's shy, I think it's because she's suffering from anxiety or some other form of annoyance that keeps her from responding well to friendliness.

Anyway, she went to the doctor when she noticed that she was putting on weight in her stomach. The reason, it turned out, was that she had growing in there a huge cancer on her uterus. It was the size of a grapefruit, and the doctor didn't think she had much chance of living.

But with chemotherapy and radiation, the cancer began to shrink. Today, it's in remission, and she's still working. She's also much more friendly these days. I think being so sick has made her reconsider her outlook on life. Anyway, instead of being grumpy, she's now quite warm and cordial. I have said the following prayer for her to protect her from further illness. (While she used to be quite heavy, now she's thin and quite attractive. So all has not been bad news.)

*Here is your child,*
*The daughter of Ku and Kane,*
*Come to ask protection*
*From illness that is caused by evil spirits.*

*Amakua, come to me and protect* [say the person's
    name]
*From death and pain and illness,*
*And bring health and good feelings to* [say the
    person's name].

*Amakua, I call on you*
*From the seas and the heavens*
*The earth and the volcanoes*
*To come here and protect* [say the person's name]
    *from sickness.*
*Keep the evil away and bring health to* [say the
    person's name].

### Healing for Vision

There are two of us at the office for which this prayer for
restored vision is important. One is myself, and the other
is a wonderful man who is having trouble with his eyes
and is having laser surgery on both of them.

My eye, my left one, suddenly started getting detritus
in front of it not so long ago. So I went to the eye doctor,
and he told me it was at the stage before a detached retina.
I was horrified, but not afraid. I believe strongly in God
and his power to heal anything that happens to me.

Meanwhile, my friend at the office has blood swirling,
like the detritus, in front of his right eye, and he must have
surgery to remove this clotting before the actual laser
surgery he needs can be done. So I said the following
prayer for us both (we both have the same eye doctor) and
our cures have been enhanced. My eye is fine again, and
the detached retina never materialized. It healed. And my
friend is going to be okay.

*O Kane and Ku, heal the vision of* [say the
    person's name]
*Which is in need of care.*

*By the populo plant, which heals, let the vision come*
    *clear*
*And the world be seen again with clarity.*

*Grant* [say the person's name] *healthy eyes*
*And take away the evil spirits*
*That have brought sickness here.*
*Let the populo do its work,*
*And the vision be healed.*

### To Heal a Broken Bone

I have a friend who was in a terrible car accident and needed my help in the form of a spell. He had been riding on a wintery, rainy day on the Beltway around Washington, when the rain suddenly turned to ice and his car skidded at sixty miles per hour.

The car plunged along the throughway, skidding from side to side, and finally came to a halt against the road divider. The hood of the car was pushed up and the side of the car on the driver's side was crushed. Since my friend was the driver, he was terribly injured.

He broke his left leg and his left arm as well as his pelvis. The ambulance took him to the hospital, and he went right away into X-ray. He called me from the hospital as he knew I could probably help him, and he described his injuries to me.

I got out several books of chants and spells for broken bones and chose the two presented here as the appropriate answer to the situation.

I went to the hospital and took some powdered Ti leaves with me. They grow in Hawaii and are much used in magical operations. Ti is a noble plant, its leaves worn on wedding days as crowns on the head.

I found my friend's hospital room, where he was lying in casts and traction with a weight hanging over the end of the bed to keep his leg stretched so that the pelvis wouldn't move. I kissed him and told him to concentrate his effort on feeling the bones heal and his body whole again. I said I would do the same thing as I sprinkled his body with powdered Ti leaves. We concentrated on his wellness and I chanted:

*Heal your bones and knit them tight.*
*May you walk with God in the light.*

Then I lit a candle and told him to concentrate on the flame as we both chanted the spell. While chanting, we both had to keep in our mind's eye an image of him healed and well, and I cast great emotion at him behind the spell.

Then I sprinkled some of the powdered Ti leaves in the flame of the candle and continued to chant.

After about fifteen minutes of this ceremony. I brought out my Hawaiian chant to heal broken bones. While sprinkling him with powdered Ti leaves, I chanted the following prayer:

*Take away the pain in the bones,*
*O Great Spirit of the heavens and the earth and the*
   *seas.*
*Bring healing here and knit the bones together*
*So that* [say the person's name] *may be well*
   *again.*

*Take the evil away that has caused this illness*
*And bring wholeness to* [say the person's name].

*O great Kane and Ku, and Pele of the volcanoes,*
*Hear my prayer and act on it.*

## To Restore Life

In the hospital, a man in very bad condition was in the bed next to my friend. While I was doing the ceremony over my friend to heal him, I noticed that the man's spirit left him.

Before the nurses were called, I sprinkled powdered Ti leaves on his bed and called to him: "Mr. Long, Mr. Long, come back in your body again. Your wife misses you. Your son misses you. Your friends miss you. Return, return." I called to him because I knew his soul was floating somewhere near the bed and he could still hear me. When you're newly dead, there's a moment when you soul hovers near your body and can be attracted back. I said to him: "Think your consciousness back in your body. Think it back and it will come back."

There was no response from him, but I had the chant with me for restoring life to a dead body.

The Hawaiians believe that the soul leaves the body through the foot. A man's soul leaves through his right foot, and a woman's through her left. In fact, they specifically believe it leaves through the big toe. There is a small school of thought, however, that believes the soul leaves through the corner of the eye, but most Kahunas agree that the toe is the place from which the soul leaves the body.

What you are supposed to do, if you can, is wrap the body in sweet-smelling flowers to attract the soul back. I had powdered Ti leaves with me for the healing ceremony for my friend, so that had to do.

I put my candle that I brought for the healing ceremony by the bedside of the newly dead man and began my chant:

> *Bring back life to this* [man/woman] *who lies here*
> *before you,*
> *Great Spirit of the Living and the dead.*
> *Amakua, draw near and bring the breath of life*
> *Back to this person who lies before you in death.*
> *Do not take this* [man's/woman's] *mana from him*
> *And leave him to die alone.*

*Bring back life and love to the limbs of this* [man/
   woman]
*That he may ride the seas and walk the sands again.*

*Great Kane and Ku, draw near to this case of death
   and restore life here.*
*Great Heavens, great earth, great oceans,*
*I call unto you.*
*Bring back the soul of this* [man/woman].
*Bring it here at once.*

The man in the bed stirred and sat up. He rubbed his
eyes and said he had dreamed he'd been dead and that I'd
called him back. I told him he was right and that he
shouldn't sleep for at least an hour until he got his
strength back. So we talked for an hour and then he
drifted away. It was just by chance I was there and that the
spell worked so well.

### To Bless the House

Hawaiians often have Kahunas bless the houses in which
they live. When a new building goes up in Honolulu, for
instance, it is traditional to have a Kahuna say a prayer
over it to keep out evil spirits. Thus it is with the private
home. You can actually have a minister say the prayers; it
doesn't have to be a real Kahuna.

My friend is moving from a house to a small apartment where she'll have many more services to take care of
her. She doesn't want evil spirits from the last tenant or
from others in the building to haunt the new apartment,
so she's going to have a minister come and say a prayer
over it. I'm going to help her cleanse the premises before
the prayers are said.

I'll take a fresh bulb of garlic and go to each corner of
her new apartment. I'll put a clove in each corner and say

"Oh, evil spirits, out and stay away from here." The garlic, which must be peeled, frightens spirits away. They cannot stand garlic and flee from it.

Then, for the ceremony for the house, there must be an offering of fish and coconut milk. The fish should be raw and the coconut milk fresh. These are offerings to the gods to bless the house and should be disposed of after the ceremony without eating them.

Have the minister come and stand in the doorway of the house or apartment. Have him face inward to say the prayer once, then outward to say it again. It is best if if you know this minister as she may be hesitant to say an Hawaiian prayer. But it's legitimate, so go ahead and ask.

Here is the prayer for the minister to say over the apartment or house that you're moving into:

> *O spirits of earth, and air and fire and water,*
> *Come to these dwellings*
> *And bless them with your mana.*
> *Take the mana from those gathered here for this*
> *    prayer*
> *And let it be generated in the dwelling for all time.*
> *Let power reside here,*
> *And the good spirits that the Great Spirit sends to*
> *    help us.*
> *Let good luck descend here,*
> *And let happiness come into the air and earth and*
> *    fire and water of this place.*
> *Let the Amakua come here*
> *And bless this place with mana and good fortune,*
> *And let the people who live here be happy and*
> *    healthy and full of life and love.*
> *Let the spirit of this place be one of joy and*
> *    goodness,*
> *And let there be peace here always.*

## *To Avert Suicide*

Some of my readers have written me in very depressed states indeed. I want to relate the story of one of them and what we did to rectify the situation.

Anne wrote that she was an alcoholic who had gotten very depressed under the influence of the drug. She decided that she wanted to take her own life, so she set about putting her affairs in order. She subscribed to the publi cation of The Hemlock Society (an organization that believes in euthanasia and in death with dignity) and learned what pills she needed to take and where to get them.

She flew to Mexico and saw a Mexican doctor who gave her prescriptions for the suicide medications she'd need. Then she came back to the United States with her medicine in her handbag.

She went around seeing people that she knew and loved for the last time, and then she went out and got very drunk. She drank ten martinis and stumbled out of the bar to go home to take her medicine.

On the way home, she passed a church and went in. She prayed for God to give her a miracle and save her life, but she was so depressed she didn't think anything that happened in church would help her. But when she got home, she saw a copy of my book and found a way to get in touch with me. I talked to her and gave her the following spell to do to avert suicide and depression.

Take a white candle and sit on the floor in the middle of your living room. Light the candle and spend a long time looking into the flame. Let your thoughts drift and quiet themselves, then concentrate on God. Picture God. Make Him the image of a friend or your parent. Concentrate on the image. It can be an image of someone close to you or a religious picture of Jesus Christ. Whoever you've chosen, keep the image in your mind and chant:

*Take me by the hand, O Spirit.*
*Move across the miles*
*From the deep of the oceans and the skies and the*
   *earth*
*And cradle me in your arms.*
*Great Spirits of Hawaii, come to me here*
*And surround me with your healing power.*

*Great power of God and the Lord Jesus,*
*Surround me now and protect me.*
*Keep me safe from my own harmful hand*
*And take away the suicidal thoughts that plague my*
   *mind.*
*Bring me peace and healing, O spirits.*

*I call out to you in this time of dire need and*
   *danger,*
*That you surround me with your power and healing*
   *love.*
*Bring me back to life and love and joy and peace.*
*Amen.*

## To Bring Peace to the House

I work with a young woman who has taken on a terrible responsibility with her marriage. She's living in a house with her new husband who looks after a houseful of elderly people. They pay the husband to look after them, and my friend, Anne, is now involved with their care, too.

She works all day at a fairly demanding job, and then goes home to cook for five or six people every night. She has to do the shopping, cooking, and housecleaning, and her husband does the moving around of the elderly people and taking them to their doctor appointments and the like.

Anne was the interloper, and the elderly people resented her from the start. One woman would walk up to her and practically spit in her face, she was so hostile. And the uncle who owns the house they all live in began to go off half-cocked. Being in his eighties, he decided he needed a girlfriend and got one because of his money.

This woman set about trying to take the old man's money away from him, and she was doing a pretty good job when I came on the scene. This woman got the old man to spend his pension on her, and the bills started going unpaid. So Anne got very perturbed and asked me if there were a spell for a situation like this.

I said I thought we needed to get rid of the new girlfriend as she seemed to be the source of most of the trouble. The finances had to be straightened out. So I suggested a spell to get rid of the other woman, period. One has to be careful with this spell as we don't want it to backfire and have the uncle enamored with Anne after getting rid of the girlfriend.

I suggested that Anne take some food from the plate of the girlfriend the next time she came to dinner—after she'd eaten from it. This would be the magical connection to the woman as the food would have touched her lips. Then Anne was to take the food, put it in a pan and heat it for the uncle's dinner. She was to put oregano in it and some black pepper, and while adding the spices she was to say:

> Woman, woman go away,
> Leave us in peace
> And stay away.
> Leave [mention his name] by himself again.
> Do this on the count of ten.

Then start counting slowly to ten. At the count of ten, quickly serve the food to the man. While adding the oregano and pepper, picture the woman's face and summon huge emotion to throw at the image. The emotion should be negative, like "get away from me" feelings.

This is a French spell; should it not work on the first try, do it again. You might save some of the food from the plate to use a second time if the woman doesn't come to dinner often. If she does, then just repeat the performance. The spell should work in a few weeks, so if you want to repeat it, do so only after two weeks pass.

### A Fetish for Good Luck

Ray is a dreamer, big time. All his waking hours are spent dreaming impossible dreams that have no hope of being turned into reality. You must dream things that can come true based on your efforts to make them do so. If you just want to pretend you're going to hit the lottery, that's not very practical.

Ray is a close friend of mine, however, and I decided to help him with his dreams. He wants a big car, a big house, and a big yacht and to become a Hollywood movie producer, but he works in public relations and has not a prayer of making it to Hollywood at the rate he's going.

One day Ray asked me for a spell that would help him with his dreams. I gave him the ESAU Square spell (from my first book) to help him. What you do is write the following spell on parchment paper with either a black pen or blood drawn from a pricked finger (the more powerful of the two methods).

$$
\begin{array}{cccc}
E & S & A & U \\
S & & & A \\
A & & & S \\
U & A & S & E
\end{array}
$$

Put the square under your pillow at night and pray on it and your luck should change for the better. So I gave

Ray this spell to do and he said that his luck was changing but that he needed something more powerful for his dreams of riches.

So I told Ray about the Obeah spell I have.

The Africans who were brought to Charleston, South Carolina, brought the Obeah with them from their native lands. One of the good luck charms that Africans used were fetishes, or grisgris bags of objects that brought luck.

Some items that bring luck and go into grisgris bags are a cap, a serpent, a monkey, a tortoise, a tree, a root, a plant, a stone with a hole in it, a cockle shell, a bunch of feathers, a tooth, parings from fingernails, hair from one's head, and a root image of an animal or man. You wrap these in a scarf, also lucky to you, and carry it about. The Africans wore their grisgris about their wrists or waists, but you may carry yours in your handbag or pocket.

The fetish is a good luck object that has mana (as they say in Hawaii) in it. It has a special power. Now tell me how cultures a world away (Hawaii and Africa) came up with the same concept belief in the concept of mana or power in an object.

Wear or carry your grisgris bag wherever you go. Caress the items when they bring you good luck, and curse them when they don't correct bad luck. That's how the Africans treat their grisgris, and so should you.

A fetish for good luck can be made of many good luck items or just one or two. It depends on what you find that's good luck for you. The items I've listed aren't the only fetish items that bring good luck, so keep your eyes open for anything that has mana.

### About the ESAU Square

The ESAU Square is my favorite spell. It's a very powerful and ancient spell from the Middle East. One of my

readers used the ESAU Square on four separate occasions
and had some concerns about it that I will address.

The first time she used the square her boyfriend was
the recipient. He was in a terrible car accident a week
before Christmas, leaving him with a severed aorta. The
doctors stitched him up, but told her that he was in very
serious condition and that if he recovered it would be two
weeks before he was out of the hospital. My witch reader
went home and did the ESAU Square without ever having
used it before. Her boyfriend not only recovered splen-
didly, but was out of the hospital in three days, two days
before Christmas. She says that the ESAU Square saved
his life.

The second time she used the square, she wanted to
get back with another boyfriend who had broken up with
her. She did the ESAU Square again, and it backfired. Her
boyfriend refused all advances that she made and
wouldn't see her again. She went back to look at the square
and discovered she had left off one of the letters. No
wonder it backfired!

Another time she used it to get money for a gown she
wanted. It didn't look promising as she didn't have the
money herself and her mother had refused to give it to
her for such a frivolous reason. Then the power of the
ESAU Square came into play and an aunt, whom she
hadn't seen in awhile, came for a visit. The aunt heard
about her desire for the dress and bought it for her. The
ESAU Square had worked again in a matter of two weeks.

The fourth time the square was used, my reader wrote
to me. It had been three days and no results were to be
had. She didn't tell me what she wished for, but only wrote
to say that it hadn't worked so far and she was afraid it
wouldn't.

I'm afraid it didn't work either (although I never
found out) because you must have faith that your spells,

once you do them, will work. If you lack faith, then the chances of them working are very slim indeed.

Other questions my reader had about the ESAU Square are as follows:

*How many times are you allowed to use the Square?* The answer is as many times as you need to. There is no limit on the number of times it can be used.

*Does it matter what one uses to get blood from the left hand?* You should use blood from the ring finger of your left hand and use a needle (clean and sterilized) to prick it. In witchcraft, always use a needle, not a pin, as the power of the head of the pin to block the magic is powerful.

*Does it matter how you clean your hand after?* No it doesn't. Use alcohol or iodine on the pin prick to make sure that it doesn't become infected. And, of course, wash your hands with soap and water to make sure they're clean.

*What do you do with the parchment paper after it is used in making the Square?* You can sleep on it, if you like, but keep it in a safe place until the spell is accomplished. Then, perform a little ceremony where you burn the Square and parchment once the spell has come to pass.

### For a Trial

Sometimes I hear from men in prison who want spells to get out. I can do that, but first we need a spell that's in effect during the trial.

James was a bartender in the Bronx. One night he was at his bar, which happened to be empty, when three men entered and tried to rob him at gunpoint. Instead of giving them the money, James pulled out a gun from behind the bar and shot and killed all three of them amid a lot of gunfire.

Then James called his boss to come get the gun, and after the gun was secured he called the police. I'm not sure what James told the police, but he certainly said that he was an innocent bystander.

The police didn't believe him, of course, and arrested him. James languished in jail for a while until his trial came up. Since I knew him and knew the story, I decided to help him.

What I did was first visit the crime scene, which was back to normal by then, and do a cleansing ceremony. I took rose water and garlic with me and, while the bar was empty, sprinkled rose water around the room with the following chant:

> *Ghosts from hell,*
> *Follow my spell*
> *And leave this place*
> *Nevermore to come back.*

Then I put garlic in all the corners of the room where the shooting took place, and the room was effectively cleansed of all ghosts that might interfere with James's trial.

Then the trial began. Since the large city newspapers didn't have an account of the trial, I arranged for a small local paper to give me copies of the proceedings. I didn't actually have to go to the Bronx to do this Obeah spell.

Take a newspaper account of the trial and put it under a fresh, white candle. Light the candle while the trial is going on and let it burn down. Replace the candle with a new one, lighting it with the flame from the old, but blow it out when the trial is not in progress. This should be done during the whole trial until it is settled. Preferably the defendant should do it himself, but he can get a friend to do it for him. I did it for James since he couldn't get a candle in jail.

While doing the spell, picture the judge and the outcome of the trial as being positive. Throw huge emotion of love at the candle and at the image of the judge in your mind.

A word of caution: If the newspaper account doesn't contain a mention of the charge against the defendant or the defense lawyer's name, then tie a piece of paper with the missing information on it to the candle and let it burn when it comes up.

The charges will be voided by the end of the trial if the spell is done properly, as it was in James's case; he was set free.

### To Shorten a Prison Term (No. 1)

John and I have had some correspondence. He's in prison for robbing a bank. He's read my books and wants a spell to get out of jail.

It seems that John was a very fancy bank robber. He covered his head with a bandanna and his eyes with a mask. He pulled a loaded gun and went into a bank where he held up one of the tellers. The teller gave him all the money she had and a bag of money with red dye in it, though John didn't know that.

When he got home, he opened the bag and the red dye got all over him, especially his face and hands. That's how he was caught because eventually he had to go out, the police saw the red dye, and he was nabbed literally red-handed as the bank robber.

John got twenty years for his efforts, and he had done six when I heard from him. I promised to help him with a spell to lower the number of years he was spending in jail. Here's what I told him to do:

First you must cleanse your cell of bad mana and evil spirits. You do this by sprinkling garlic powder around the cell floor (especially in the corners), and saying the following chant:

*Garlic, garlic cleanse the air,*
*Keep the atmosphere here fair.*
*If the spirits try to stay,*
*Scare them away.*

Then sprinkle more garlic powder around, and you're ready for the next step.

After the premises have been cleansed and all the bad mana and evil spirits are gone, take a piece of paper, clean and white, and a pigeon feather with a quill still on it, and prick your ring finger. Using a drop of blood, use the quill to draw a small arrow with a shaft and head on the paper. You don't need to draw the feathers. Then take another drop of blood and write your initials at the tip of the arrow.

When the paper is dry, fold it in four squares and sleep on it for ten nights. But before you do that, do the following chant over it:

*Blood and feather,*
*Write my name on the sky*
*And bring me freedom*
*Like the arrow in my blood.*

Now sleep on the paper for ten nights, and picture yourself in a state of freedom before going to bed each night. Also say the Lord's Prayer.

At the end of the ten nights, take the paper and burn it to ash. Sprinkle the ash around the prison cell floor (especially in the corners) and chant:

*Freedom for me*
*Let there be.*
*Let me fly away*
*From this place.*

Your prison sentence should be reduced sometime in the next six months, and it should be by a substantial amount.

### To Shorten a Prison Term (No. 2)

One of my dear readers is a woman who has met a man who is in prison. She has been writing to him and he to her. But recently, he was moved from one prison to another further away where she can't visit him, and he's stopped writing.

When she visited him—they were introduced through a mutual friend—they immediately fell in love. She would see him and he would be happy that she did. They were very happy together, she thought. Then he moved.

Since he's been gone, he hasn't written to her. She's afraid he's forgotten their love, and she's desperate. She doesn't want to be forgotten by him, so she's asked me if there's a spell to help keep someone in mind. Here it is:

Take a ruby red candle and put beside it a red stone. It can be a piece of glass or a coral rock or a real ruby or whatever you have that's red and is similar. Put a picture of your beloved under the red stone. Light the candle and concentrate on the flame; get a good picture of your lover in your mind's eye. That should be easy to do with his picture in front of you. Now send waves of love from your heart along your left arm to your fingertips. Touch the red stone, and it will magnify the love waves you're sending. Now reverse the waves of love and send them into your brain into the picture you're holding of him there. Do this reversal of power three times.

He won't forget you and will contact you shortly by letter.

Now to the prison situation. This will have to be a long-distance spell that I recommend, as my reader's lover has moved to a prison far away. But with witchcraft, distance isn't a factor. You can do a spell on someone on the West Coast just as easily as from the East or the West Coast.

You need to make a guffah bag of yellow silk with a yellow satin ribbon around the top. In the guffah bag you put a blue stone (glass will do), a yellow feather, and a sprinkle of powder. You need to put in a penny—a shiny new one. (Go to the bank, they'll give you a new one.) Put these items in the bag, and while you're doing it chant:

> *Prison bars come down for me,*
> *Let* [mention his name] *be set free.*

> *Prison bars come down for me,*
> *Let* [mention his name] *be close to me.*

Now carry the guffah bag with you for a period of a month until the next full moon. You can keep it in your handbag, or, better yet, wear it around your waist. Be sure you visualize him when you say the chant. Also, say the chant over the bag about once a week as you caress the bag and try to make it work for you. Before a parole hearing or other time when there's the possibility he might be set free is the best time to do this spell. It will help the process go his way.

### *Financial Independence*

John Jefferson works in the legislative division of the American Legion, and he makes a good but modest salary. He wants financial independence, which he defines as having enough money to be comfortable. He isn't materialistic and doesn't need a Mercedes Benz, for example. But he would like to put his wife through college (she helped him through and worked while he studied). He also would like to eventually be able to send his daughter to college and finance his son's education in a good school, too. Those are his dreams, not a big house or fancy clothes. He also would like to be able to set his mother up with a nicer place to live before she's too old to enjoy it.

John Jefferson is an admirable young man and is willing to work to gain financial independence. He can write well, so I'm encouraging him to write a book. He wants to write one about his experiences, but doesn't know how to organize it. So I'm helping him with that. If he finishes it, I will help him try to find a publisher.

There are a variety of spells you can use to gain enough money to live comfortably. One of the best is the ESAU Square I wrote about some pages ago. It's a powerful charm and I've given it to John, but he wants something more potent. He wants a spell he can chant to make it work. So I'm going to provide two spells for John. One is an amulet and the other is an Obeah spell.

Put in a little gold silk sack—which you make using gold thread around the top to secure it—the following items: A penny with a hole in it (use a drill to make the hole), a dash of salt, and a piece of garlic.

Wear the sack as a juju bag by carrying it in your pocket or keeping it in your purse. Keep it with you at all times; finger the material from time to time and concentrate on images of great wealth. Remember, you have to start a business or be situated in the work world where you can make money in order for the charm to work. It's no good to think you're going to hit the lottery and just sit back and do nothing.

The other spell, the Obeah one, I've found for John to do is as follows:

Put a dollar bill and some seeds from a tangerine into a pot with some dirt. As the plant grows, say over it each day the following chant:

*Grow money grow,*
*Grow as the plant grows,*
*Grow in power and wealth.*
*Grow in my pocket.*
*Grow in my hand.*
*Grow like a million*
*Grains of sand.*

While chanting over the plant with the dollar bill in it, picture great wealth surrounding you. Imagine yourself in a lovely home with a happy family around you, free from want and able to do everything you want to do. Keep the image in your mind for at least two minutes as you chant over your plant and tend and water it. When it grows as much as it will grow inside, take it outside in the summer and plant the whole pot in the ground. Your wealth should come upon you as you work toward your goal.

### To Fight Evil Influences

My friend Jim Butler knows a man who is a fisherman. This fisherman lives in Maryland on the ocean where he has his fishing business to keep body and soul together.

He has a trawler, and he and his son do a pretty good job of hauling in fish to make a living. They use a seine, which is a large net that drifts for hundreds of yards across a fishing ground. Then the boat comes around the net and hauls in the fish. It's made out of twine and is sturdy, though it can still break and needs mending now and then.

The fishing business is highly competitive, and Jim's friend has two or three other fishermen with whom he competes for the fish in the area. He usually gets the biggest catch, and this makes the other men jealous. So it came as no surprise to Jim's friend that they'd try something to keep him from having his usual good luck in the fish-hauling area.

The three fishermen who compete with Jim's friend got together and hired a witch to put a spell on him. The spell worked and soon Jim's friend started having unusual amounts of trouble with his seine. It kept ripping, and the fish didn't seem as plentiful when he hauled it in. Soon, his fishing business was dwindling to nothing, and Jim's friend asked what could be done about it. Jim asked me if I knew of a counterspell that could ward off the evil one the witch had put on his friend and his son. I said I'd help.

What I recommended was an Obeah spell, as the witch in Maryland practiced Obeah, too. Jim's friend found out that the fisherman had hired her from a friend to whom they had bragged about the spell. So they weren't shy about letting people know what they'd done.

I told Jim I would have to do the spell myself to counteract the witch who had put this evil spell on his friend. It was actually put on his boat, I determined, from the amount of trouble he was having with his net. So I went down to the shore and performed the following ceremony on the boat:

I took three shells and wrote the names of the three fishermen who had asked for the charm on them. I used a felt-tipped marker so the names could be easily seen. Then I took three fish and gutted them and put the shell inside. I took a pinch of guffah dust from a nearby graveyard (from the grave of a local fisherman) and put some inside each of the fish. I took the fish to the boat and put one in the bow and one in the stern and one in the middle of the boat. Then I chanted:

*Break the spell that's cast this way,*
*Return it to the ones where it came from.*

*Do this spirits I pray,*
*May the magic rebound on them.*

The spell should start working at once. The spell that was put on Jim's friend came off immediately. He started having good luck right away, and the three men went back to their usual secondary position in the fishing competition.

## To Guard Against Drugs

Jeff is a young drug addict who has had an experience that has made him want to give it up. I'm helping him.

He had the experience about a year ago when he went to Thailand. He was high on drugs and decided on the spur of the moment to take a train into the highlands. He got on a train and rode all day and into the night. About midnight he heard himself say, "This is it, get out here." The train came to a place high in the mountains where it slowed to a crawl. Jeff went between the cars with his bag (a roll of cloth) and jumped off the train in the middle of nowhere in the middle of the night. He began walking, and toward dawn he saw a path.

He took the pathway and it led to a tiny village. He spoke some Thai, but not the dialect of the village, so he was effectively cut off from everyone. The villagers fed him, however, when he indicated he was hungry, and gave him a place to stay in one of their homes.

In the home where he was staying was a young Thai woman who was very beautiful. She immediately took it upon herself to wait on Jeff. He taught her his name, and she taught him hers. He spent several weeks there getting to know this girl and the language as much as he could. And he told the elder of the village that he wanted to marry this girl.

The village elder agreed, and the couple, who were in love and happy, got married in the village in a local ceremony. Jeff lived an idyllic life without drugs up there in the mountains, but knew he'd have to return to the United States to his job before long. He wanted to take his new wife with him, and he was afraid he'd start using drugs again.

I met Jeff after his return some months later. He had brought his simple, country bride with him to the big city. He was terrified of drug use and knew he had to guard against it in every way possible. I told him we'd make a fetish for him to guard against it.

We took a red bandanna that I purchased on the street and put in it a piece of bone (chicken), feathers (chicken or pigeon), ashes of watercress, and a wood carving of a bird. I tied the bandanna with the objects in it and gave it to Jeff to carry in his pocket or wear around his waist.

Before giving it to him, however, I chanted over it:

> *Charm do not break.*
> *A strong spell make*
> *For health and wealth*
> *And happiness of the wearer.*

This is an Obeah fetish and brings the wearer health, wealth, and happiness if carried in the proper manner. Put it in your pocket if you're a man or wear it around your waist; put it in your purse, if you're a woman, or around your waist. Caress the outside of the fetish when your luck is good, and curse it when it's bad. It should keep you from desiring drugs as long as you wear it properly.

### *To Divine Dreams*

An eighteen-year-old friend of mine has a story to tell. She's in love with a young man who only wants to be her friend. The two were friends and shared many interests until they went to a computer dating service that her school held for a fund-raiser. The dating service said they were perfectly matched, and that's when my young friend became more interested in him than as just a friend.

There was a long, awkward stage when my friend and the fellow didn't speak to each other very much. A third friend told him that the girl was interested in him and then told her that the fellow was interested in her. That only served to make matters worse and pushed them further apart. This situation existed either because they really didn't care much for each other, or because they cared for each other too much and were too shy. But anyway, they lost their friendship for a good long while.

Then they started, gradually, becoming friends again. This time, my young friend told me, she wanted to just be friends with him and nothing more. So she concentrated on that. But I think she was really in love with him.

Then she had several dreams. They were lucid dreams (which means they were very clear and real seeming), and I repeat them here.

The first dream involved the young man driving her home in a red sports car. He told her to put a tape in the tape deck and she did, saying it was her favorite tape. His eyes bulged out and the car slowed. It pulled up to the house that she had lived in when she was seven years old. She was carrying many boxes and bags, and when she got out the young man came around and helped her. Then he kissed her passionately. He got back in his car and left.

The second dream came toward morning and went as follows:

She was standing in front of her locker at school in an empty hallway. She heard footsteps behind her, and, when she turned to look to see who was there, she saw the young man. He ignored her, got a book about Leonardo DaVinci out of his locker, and went outside. He brought a stray, pregnant, white dog into the building and gave her food, then came over to see my friend. He kissed her and said, "See you in class," and walked away. She spun in circles in the hallway until the bell rang, which was actually her alarm clock going off.

The spell to divine a dream is fairly simple, but must be accomplished with a lot of attention. What you do is sit in front of a mirror with a candle in a bowl. Drop a small pinch of rosemary on the candle flame and look deep into your mirror-image eyes. While doing this, clear your mind of all stray thoughts and let your consciousness drift. As the rosemary burns, the meaning of the dream will come to you in your mind's eye. It may be a picture or a sentence, but you'll somehow get the message of the meaning of the dream. Before you burn the rosemary, repeat the dream you want divined in your mind so it's fresh and your subconscious and witchcraft will know what you want to know.

The beauty of this spell is that you find out right away what your dream meant to you. It could be something totally unrelated. If you have a vision of the two of you kissing, then that's the meaning of the dream. My friend had this vision. She found out she was still in love with him and that they weren't just friends.

### To Help Another

Joanne wrote me about her life and her family. She needs help for herself as well as others in her family, but she only writes about wanting to help her mother.

Her mother worked as a maid all her life to raise her two girls. She always hoped they'd do better than she did in life and wanted an education for Joanne so that she could get a good job. Joanne's sister got pregnant twelve years ago and had to get married. She married an abusive man and is now afraid to get a divorce in case he does something to her or, takes the two girls she's had away from her.

Joanne herself thinks she ruined her life five years ago when she got pregnant, too. Her mother's dreams for her went down the tubes and she became a full-time mom. She also married, which was hard because they didn't get along well. But the main tragedy was that her child was born with cerebral palsy and needs constant care and attention. He's fed by tubes, and Joanne is tied to him. Yet Joanne's concern is for her mother's happiness. She thinks she let her mother down and that her mother is unhappy because of this.

Joanne had another little girl about two years ago, and she is normal and a joy in her life. So is her son with cerebral palsy, but in a different way. Joanne must have a very large heart indeed to be so concerned for her mother's happiness with all the problems she has.

I decided to help Joanne, who wants to start a home business with her sister so they can make money to better their lives. I decided this was something I could do to help them, and also cast a spell for their mother's happiness.

For helping another (her mother) I recommend the following spell. It's an Obeah spell, and uses a guffah bag to bring good luck to the other person.

Put in a white silk sack the following items: black-eyed peas (you can use canned or dried), two white pigeon feathers, a sprinkle of baby powder or face powder, and a wood carving of a bird. Take the guffah bag and bury it near the front doorstep of the person's house you're trying to help. Before you bury it, however, chant over it:

> *Luck to* [mention the person's name],
> *Bring luck to* [him/her].

*Catch the sun and place it in this house*
*So that the dark may not come here.*

Then bury it after visualizing the person you're doing the spell for and summoning love emotions.

To help Joanne with her business, I did the following French spell:

*Money come here and stick*
*To the fingers of* [mention the person's
    name].
*May* [his/her] *business thrive and do well*
*And may the curse of darkness*
*Be far away from* [him/her].

Visualize and cast the emotions of happiness and love at the person you're helping. It also helps to picture her as a successful businessperson so that the engrams of the situation are placed in the consciousness of the world. Have the person who is starting the business visualize herself as successful at it too. And say the chant three times over a period of two weeks to help them get started.

### For a Quick Reply

Jonathan wrote me that he had a need for a spell to get a quick reply to a letter. He was posted in Asia with the State Department and wrote to his girlfriend asking her to marry him. He didn't hear from her for quite some time. So he wrote me to see if there's a spell to get her to answer him quickly.

I myself have had need of such a spell. I have a book manuscript that I need an agent for, and I need it to be read quickly and accepted or rejected with dispatch so that I can find someone who will accept it. I can't afford to wait weeks and weeks while the manuscript sits in a pile of others waiting for a reply.

Emil needs to have a quick reply to questions in letters that he's sent out. He sent one of the letters to me for a quick response, and it just sat there for weeks. I didn't have time to get to it, and he had need of a spell during that whole time I sat on it.

The correct spell to get an answer to a letter promptly is to take the letter you're sending and rub it with a pumice stone from Hawaii. Pumice comes from volcanoes; you can get it in the drug store as it removes callouses from your feet and hands. Rub the letter with a pumice stone and say, as you're doing this:

> *Pumice of Pele,*
> *Light a fire under the feet of* [say the person's name]
> *So that he'll send me my reply immediately.*

You should hear within two weeks of writing your letter.

## To Remove a Spell

Daniele came to me one afternoon with a hair-raising story. She said she had been to a palm reader who read her palm for five dollars and told her she had a spell on her. It would cost twenty-five dollars to have it removed.

I told Daniele this was a come-on to get her to spend money, but she insisted the woman was right because her finances were not in order and the curse was on her financial house. She said that her in-laws from Jamaica had pulled some hair out of her head some months ago and that she knew they had done a spell with it.

Daniele also said she was having nightmares. She had

told this to the palm reader and the woman told her this was part of the spell. She said what she must do to get rid of the nightmares is to go to a tree, any tree, tell the tree the nightmares' content, then throw a quarter over her left shoulder. This would remove the curse of the nightmares. I believed this Obeah ritual would work and told Daniele it would.

Then I gave her the following Obeah spell to remove the curse on her finances.

Make a guffah bag of a penny with a hole in it, some black-eyed peas to ward off the evil eye, and a bird feather (any bird will do) to ensure the spell will have wings and work. Tie the items in a green silk purse with green thread at the top and carry it around for a month, until the next full moon. Then bury the purse in your backyard by the light of the full moon, and the spell should be removed.

You must have faith that this spell will work; touch and fondle the guffah bag every day.

### To Help With School

I have a very tearful letter from a young woman in her thirties who is trying to go back to school. She's studying to be a nurse and has tried everything. I quote from her letter:

"I've tried my hardest to get good grades, I have even had tutors. But nothing really seems to work. I have also tried hypnosis on good study habits and memory concentration, but it doesn't work. I'm at the point where I feel I have a brain disorder. I've tried your spell and carry the walnut with me every day and still get Fs and Ds. Am I hopeless or has someone put a hex on me? I also use flash cards and tape record my notes, and I feel I know my exams, but when I get my tests back the scores are low, Fs and Ds. Please help me. This is what I've wanted to do for a long time—be a nurse."

Some people just aren't cut out to be students. It's as simple as that. But low grades could be caused by other problems. She may be taking a medication that is interfering with her memory, or she may have used drugs of some kind that ruined her memory. Or, indeed, there may be a hex on her so that she can't get good grades.

In any case, I'm going to help her with two spells. One is to help her get good grades, and the other is to take a hex off her, in case there is one that someone put on her.

The spell to get good grades goes as follows:

Go to a lakeshore and take a pebble. Skip it out over the water as far as it will go. If it sinks without skipping, keep skipping stones until they start to skip. In the same way, concentration will come to you and you'll be able to concentrate and remember. This is an Indian spell from my friend Jim.

Now, the spell to remove the hex if one has been put on you and you're unable to get good grades:

This is an Obeah spell for removing hexes in general. It involves making a guffah bag, which should include the following items: a small grinning model of a devil's face in clay; a horse nail bent in the middle; a worn horseshoe or a knife spring blade; and a short bit of soft wood with a carved head and a couple of brass tacks for eyes, with one or two red cock feathers bound around the waist of the doll with red and white strings.

Make this a very large guffah bag of black cloth with a black ribbon running around the top. It will take some time to put together and may take a trip to the country to get the ingredients, but it's worth it. The items will keep away hexes of all kinds, not just those to give you bad grades in school, so you can use the guffah bag if you feel you've been bewitched by someone.

I feel, for example, I've been bewitched as far as my job goes. I can't get another job no matter how I've tried over the last five years. I'm pretty sure I've been bewitched by someone practicing Wicca. I've recently made the guffah bag; it took me six months to put it together, but I expect the hex to be removed.

Take your guffah bag and keep it in your desk where you study or work. Keep the desk drawer locked so no one will happen upon it. Every day stroke your guffah bag and visualize success. If you want a high-paying job, visualize yourself in that position. If you want to get good grades, picture As and stroke your guffah bag. Picture yourself studying successfully, and you will break the hex. It should take about a month, until the next full moon, to work.

### To Be Liked

Jeremy was a young man who, like everyone else, wanted to be liked by others. He had difficulty, however, with this situation because he was handicapped and was awkward.

Jeremy was born with spina bifida (his spine didn't meet and left him paralyzed), and he has to use crutches and a wheelchair to get around. But the spina bifida wasn't the only handicap he had.

Jeremy had developed, at thirty, into a man who was a know-it-all. There wasn't anything that Jeremy wasn't an expert on. He was such a know-it-all that he put people off and they didn't like him as a result.

He came to me with this problem of people not liking him, and I gave him the following spell:

Take a piece of blue cloth and tie in it the following objects: a small hammer, two ten-penny nails, two cock feathers from a red rooster, a pheasant foot, and a rabbit's tail. Tie in the cloth with a blue satin ribbon. Carry it with you wherever you go for a month, then put it in a locked drawer at your office if you work or in your home if you don't. Leave it there until the next full moon, then bury it by a tall pine tree in a forest. You should have people eating out of your hand.

The chant to say when preparing the fetish is as follows:

> *Like me for who I am,*
> *Not for what I appear to be.*
> *Like me as a child of light.*
> *May these objects give you the gift of sight.*

### To Quit Smoking

This is a hard subject to deal with for witchcraft as you're dealing with an addiction that's very hard to break under ordinary circumstances. But in conjunction with other methods of giving up smoking, it can be usefully employed.

If you're like Mike, you want to help a friend give up smoking. What you must do is take his pack of cigarettes when he's not looking and carry them home with you.

Light a red candle with a match. Light each cigarette in the candle flame, and chant the following over it:

> *Burn, O evil one, in the light of God.*
> *And as you burn, so goes the need for you.*
> *Diminish the need for you,*
> *As you grow weaker and used by the flame.*
> *Diminish and die,*
> *Like the flame that consumes you.*

Do this with each cigarette from the pack, putting them out only when they burn down to the filter. Light them one right after another, and let them all burn down at the same time, or you'll be there all night. Put them in ashtrays to burn and make sure you chant over each cigarette as you light it.

When used in conjunction with a program to quit smoking, this spell should help ease the desire for cigarettes that makes people smoke.

The desire for cigarettes should diminish and disappear within two weeks of doing the chant, which is a lot shorter time than it ordinarily takes the desire to go away.

### To Find a Friend and to Get an Answer to Your Letter

I received the saddest letter from a reader who asked for my help. She sounded like she had been through a lot and maybe wasn't in the greatest mental condition. She was afraid of people not listening to her when she talked of her problems, afraid of being laughed at. She didn't trust men because of a lot of bad experiences with them, but yet she had read about a movie star who sounded exactly like what she wanted. She wanted my help to get the movie star to be sensitive to her letter to him.

I decided I could help. I can get someone to read a letter and respond. I can also do a spell to help you find a friend, or at least recommend a spell for you to find a friend. So we'll do both spells here.

But my reader has other problems. She says she lives in a dream world where people don't laugh at each other and everyone is kind. We all understand and empathize with that dream world and wish it were a reality. Maybe, with the Second Coming of Christ, it will happen, but meanwhile we need to help each other as much as possible and be as kind as we can to each other.

To my reader, here is the spell for getting someone to read your letter and take you seriously:

Use expensive paper. Most people write on notebook

paper and it doesn't stand out. Find a paper store and get quality writing paper. Use a fountain pen, not a ballpoint. This too will make an impression. And after you've written your letter, pouring out your thoughts in the clearest way possible, do the following chant over the letter:

> *Letter of hope and love,*
> *Sent to my*
> *heart's desire,*
> *Read it and answer me*
> *With love and compassion.*

When you chant over your letter, have a white candle nearby to help with concentration. Picture the person you're sending the letter to and send waves of love to your telepathic image. Let a drop of candle wax fall on the envelope and continue to picture the person as the wax drops. You should hear within a month from the person you've written to.

### Find a Friend

Pick a club or church function or some other place where people gather and go there. Carry with you a guffah bag with the following items in it: a gold charm of a face, part of a peacock feather, a sprinkle of baby powder, and a turtle shell. Put these in a white silk sack that you make and close it with white silk thread. Say over the guffah bag:

> *Friend to me,*
> *Friend to be,*
> *Come to me,*
> *Soon to me,*
> *Love me*
> *And I'll love you.*

Now carry the sack to the event you're going to, and walk up to people and start conversations. One of these people will become your friend and your troubles will be over.

## *To Change Your Looks*

There is a time when you're a teenager that the way you look is more important than anything else in your life except teens of the opposite sex.

I can recall at thirteen being humiliatingly plump and having the boys laugh at me if I expressed an interest in them that was other than just superficially friendly. I wasn't even fat at thirteen, but I can remember that my skin was oily, my hair was oily, I was plump, and I had a few pimples on my face. I was not a pretty sight. But to no one was I as ugly as I was to myself; I wanted to change my appearance completely.

I'd spend hours in front of the mirror adjusting my nose to make the tip straight (when I was actually given a chance to have plastic surgery at twenty-five, I turned it down) and trying to find the best possible angle that my face could be viewed at. I used to dream of having my picture on the cover of *Time* or *Life* and to think to myself, I'll get even for this humiliation someday.

Dreams such as these lead to great accomplishments in lots of children, I'm sure. What we dream as children very often reflects what we do later in life to fulfill ourselves.

In any case, I know a young lady who wants to completely change her looks, using witchcraft. What I can offer her is a spell to make her seem more attractive to other people, but there is nothing that will actually change the color of your eyes or hair or the shape of your face. But you can *seem* more attractive.

The object is to make you more magnetic to others,

give you some charisma. I know a young woman who has everyone hanging on her every word because she has that fine quality, charisma. Charm. She makes enemies easily, too, so you want to be sure that you use your charisma only for good, not evil.

Here is the spell you need. Make a guffah bag that contains the following items: a white feather, a piece of red silk cut in a heart shape, a new gold comb, and a new gold mirror. Put these in a white silk guffah bag that you make and string with red satin ribbon.

Chant over the guffah bag the following words:

> *Goddess of beauty,*
> *Make me yours.*
> *Bring me great beauty*
> *And great charm.*
> *Make me magnetic to the opposite sex,*
> *And make them unable to deny me anything.*

Then wear your guffah bag around your waist for a week. You can do this by wearing a blazer or suit coat over your clothes for a week and hiding the guffah bag underneath. Then take the guffah bag and lock it in a drawer in your bedroom where prying eyes won't find it. Keep it there for two weeks. After that, take it out and wear it again until the moon is full. At the full moon, take the bag off, light a white candle, and do the chant again over the bag. Then put it permanently away. Your looks should be more magnetic to the opposite sex from this point on. You should feel the change as you wear the guffah bag up to the full moon. You'll be charming!

### *To Bring Good Luck*

There's a young woman of my acquaintance, Lonnie, who has the worst luck of anyone I've ever heard of. She lost a job she loved in 1989, and her two ex-bosses wouldn't talk to her anymore. It's not that she was fired. No, they lost their business. They may have blamed her, though, as she was business manager, but she doesn't think so.

Then she got a job she didn't like just to put food on the table, and her dog died. Her boss called her at home at night and made fun of her dog dying by pretending to have sex with the dog on the phone and then sighing his name. She took him to court for this travesty.

Then she got a job as business manager in another business and was finally happy, as the job had so much responsibility. But that job ended when the Federal Bureau of Investigation came calling and the business partners were arrested for illegal activity.

Lonnie wouldn't have had any luck whatsoever if it hadn't been for bad luck.

I told her I would help her. She showed me her resumé which she sent out to 1,500 businesses around the country. It was a masterpiece. She kept getting comments, though, when anyone bothered, that she was overqualified. I just think the job market was terribly tight and no one was moving from their current jobs.

Lonnie had to sell her house and move into an apartment because of her financial situation. She was slowly drifting toward homelessness.

I gave her the following spell to bring her good luck:

Get three feathers (eagle if possible) and tie them together with black thread. Keep them separate, not bunched together, and hang them over your door. Before doing so, however, chant the following spell over them:

> *Feathers of the bird of God,*
> *Bring my dreams close to the Great Spirit.*
> *Make my luck and fortune good*
> *And full of the Great Spirit's blessing.*

*Bring me the luck of God,*
*And let the blessings of the Great Spirit*
*Be with me now and forever.*

Now with the feathers, especially if they're eagle feathers, hang a horseshoe with the points up around the feathers so the feathers sit in the middle of the horseshoe. This will attract good fortune in and of itself.

Put this fetish over your front door on the inside, and reach up and touch it every day. Stroke the feathers and say a prayer to God as you put your attention on the fetish.

Your luck should begin to change at once. Leave the fetish up at least until the full moon of the month following the one in which you put it up. You can leave it longer if you like. Keep the feathers in a safe place after you take them down, however; they may be used in other spells.

## To Get Off Welfare

Pretty soon now welfare is going to remove its safety net for a good many people. There will be thousands left without jobs and without income. This spell is for them and for others on the bottom of the economic scale who need help in succeeding.

Martha was a young woman who was on AFDC and welfare with her two fatherless children. She lived in Texas and met her third husband John down there. He had a low-paying job, but was working.

Then John was injured on his job but was able to collect worker's compensation for his injury. This was not as good as a salary, but was still okay. However, Martha couldn't collect welfare anymore, so they lived on the worker's comp until that was taken away from them in a hearing with the insurance company. So they went back on welfare.

Meanwhile, the marriage had deteriorated into a shouting match. John decided to go live with his mother and left Martha and her children. Martha was pregnant, however, so John eventually came back. But the baby was so big when he was born, he died in childbirth. She had had natural childbirth and the anesthetist had been sent home by the doctor when it looked like all was going well. But then the shoulders started out and they were too big and the baby died before the anesthetist got back to the clinic.

Martha's mother-in-law practices black witchcraft and Wicca. Martha thinks she had something to do with all this misfortune because she hates Martha and wanted her son back.

I'm not sure that Martha was the victim of Wicca or the craft, but I do know that those on the bottom of the ladder seem to fall off into deeper trouble instead of heading upward a good share of the time. Alcoholics talk of "hitting bottom," and that's often what you must do to change your life and start back in the other direction. It's something like this with poverty. You must face the reality of the bottom before you can change enough to start back up the ladder. That's what happened to Martha. She now has a full-time job, is off welfare, and is in fairly good condition. Her skirmish with the bottom brought her back up out of sheer fear and willpower—and the help of a higher power, God.

The spell to help you start on the road back to sanity and a good life is as follows:

Make a guffah bag of three feathers, a horseshoe, a sprinkle of baby powder, and a chicken bone (the wishbone if you can get it). Put these items in a white cloth and tie them at the top. Say over the guffah bag the following chant:

*Bring me luck,*
*Bring me money,*
*Bring me love,*
*O Holy Spirit.*

Picture yourself with plenty as you make the guffah bag and say the chant. Then carry it with you for as long as it takes for your luck to change. This could be days, weeks or months depending on your condition. Stroke the guffah bag every day. Bawl it out when it doesn't bring you luck, and praise it when it does on a case-by-case basis. You should get off the bottom with the aid of the guffah bag and God.

### To See the Past

One of my friends wants to be able to see into the past to find out the reason events turned out as they did. You would think that just remembering would be all that is required, but one problem is that we all forget the details that make up our story, and another is that we may not recognize the pivotal situation that influenced our story.

I'm a great believer in cause and effect. It seems to me that if you drink too much and are an alcoholic, eventually you're going to lose everything and find yourself on the street. Another cause and effect is dealing drugs. If you're a drug dealer, the chances of either winding up murdered or in jail are extremely good. But there are subtler causes and effects.

"Selfishness—self-centeredness! That, we think, is the root of our troubles. Driven by a hundred forms of fear, self-delusion, self-seeking and self-pity, we step on the toes of our fellows and they retaliate." That quote comes from the Big Book, Alcoholics Anonymous, on page 62. It tells us exactly what happens so often in our lives: Cause and effect. You're selfish to a friend or stranger, and that person responds negatively. Fear drives you to lie, and lying gets you in trouble. Cause and effect. So it goes with knowing the past.

To really know what made you a shy child, and later an alcoholic who loses everything, is worth knowing. It's easy to blame parents, but chances are there is a character flaw or peer situation that caused the shyness. Just to know would be a wonderful power. So here's a spell that helps you to find out.

Take a candle into a darkened room and sit naked on the floor in front of a full-length mirror so that you can see your own eyes. Memorize the following spell, then chant it while staring deeply into your eyes in the mirror. Hold the candle so it highlights your face.

> *Power of sun, power of earth,*
> *Power of wind, power of sky,*
> *Come to me here, evoke the past before my eyes.*
> *Let me see what caused* [Here mention what it is
>     you want to know] *from the past*
> *And let me be informed of the future consequences*
>     *that it represents.*
> *Power of God, come before me*
> *And unfold the past before my eyes*
> *So that I may know my past and future life.*

Then let your mind drift without thinking for a few seconds until an image takes shape. Whatever image you bring up is the root cause of the situation you find yourself in.

Knowing the past helped my friend, and she was able to understand why she chose a particularly destructive relationship to be in. She realized her ego needed to be all powerful in the relationship and it just wasn't. So she was able to drop the hurtful romance and join the human race again.

### *To Stop Gambling*

Betsy and Tony are lovers. He's an airline pilot, so they get to fly to a lot of different places together. His favorite place is Las Vegas.

Betsy and Tony went to Las Vegas about three months after they met. They cruised into town and headed for the hotel and casino. They took a nap and then went downstairs for some action. Tony played roulette and soon lost everything he had, about five hundred dollars. Then he asked Betsy for her money. She wouldn't give it up. He begged her, pleaded with her, but she held firm.

Then Tony told her to get on a bus and leave town if she wouldn't give him her money. So that's what she did. She went upstairs, packed, and went to the bus station. Fortunately, she only had to buy a ticket to California where she lived, so it wasn't a complete disaster.

Tony showed up at the bus station, still pleading with Betsy. She held firm. She got on the bus and went home. What Tony did she didn't know; he probably used his credit card to get more cash.

I told Betsy I'd help her because by now she was desperately in love with Tony. I told her the best thing she could have done is leave him. Gamblers are like alcoholics, they will take you down with them if you let them.

Tony is now in Gamblers Anonymous and is learning the twelve-step way to heal his addiction. But for those, like Betsy, who have loves who aren't yet enrolled, there is a spell to help gambling addicts.

What you must do, however, is get something belonging to the gambler. The best thing would be his deck of cards, if you can swing it.

Suppose you were able to get a deck of cards that belonged to him. Buy a new deck of your own. Take out all the kings from his deck and all the queens from yours. Put your four queens on top of his four kings as you chant the following chant:

> *Queen on king,*
> *King under queen.*
> *Let me rule you*
> *As woman rules man.*
> *No more gambling,*
> *Night or day.*
> *Stay away from cards*
> *And do as I say.*

Then take the cards outside to your back yard, visualizing him as you're doing it. Go to the nearest tree, dig a hole, and bury the cards there. Leave them in the ground until your gambling man gets into Gamblers Anonymous for strong help.

Tony is okay now. He doesn't go near Las Vegas anymore. He and Betsy jet here and there for happy times together. They've since married and have a small child who travels with them too. But they're very mindful that Tony is not cured. He's in remission and a slip back into gambling could ruin their lives. While five hundred dollars wasn't much for a gambler to lose, it was an indication of the fever that took him over, especially the way he treated Betsy when she stood in the way of his addiction.

### *For Shopkeepers*

There's nothing more frustrating than getting into a situation with a shopkeeper. Suppose you have your car at the mechanic's and he says it requires a coil in the heating system and it will cost $450. He says he puts it in and it still doesn't work. What's really broken is the sixteen dollar thermostat. You still have to pay for the coil. What you need is a good spell to get honest work from your car mechanic.

The grocery store is another place you could use a spell sometimes. Suppose you want an item the store doesn't carry, and you ask them to stock it. They don't want to because it's not a popular item, so you need a spell to gain cooperation at the grocery store.

And the dry cleaner loses your dress. You could get money from them to buy another one, but you really want the dress that they've lost. You need a spell to have the dress found and gain cooperation from the dry cleaner to find it.

Suppose you have a mailman who has proven to not be too reliable. The mail you're expecting sometimes gets returned to the sender without ever coming your way. You need a spell to get a reliable postman.

Suppose you had a dress made by a dressmaker and it doesn't quite fit. She fixes it and it still doesn't fit. She becomes stubborn and doesn't want to fix it anymore. You need a spell to gain your dressmaker's cooperation.

What you really need in all these cases is a spell that will gain the cooperation of shopkeepers, and keep them honest. Here is a spell from the gypsies in France that's as old as they come.

Make or buy a doll with a red-patterned skirt or pinafore. It could look like Raggedy Ann; it could even be Raggedy Ann. Now chant the following spell over the doll:

> *Shopkeeper who meets my needs,*
> *Be kind to me and do good deeds.*

*When I need special treatment,*
*Give it to me.*
*When I need special items, get them for me.*
*When I need honest work done,*
*Do it for me.*

Now take the doll and put it in your bedroom on your bed. Every day, caress the doll and hold it close. Once a week, say the chant again.

This should keep all service people with whom you have contact honest and cooperative in their dealings with you.

Another spell is to catch a frog and keep it in an aquarium. Chant over the frog the same spell as above. Once a day, caress the frog by stroking its back. This will have the same effect as the doll but may be easier to do for you country witches.

The effect of the spell is indefinite as long as you caress the doll or frog and say the spell once a week.

### For Good Health

Good health requires that you have access to good doctors and go to them when you have aches and pains and other illnesses. You must keep up with your health and not be afraid to go to the doctor when something is wrong.

Anette takes care of some elderly people in her home. One of them recently went to live with his girlfriend, and apparently she didn't feed him because he wound up dehydrated and unfed in the hospital. Anette has him back in the house again and is looking after him. He's eating again and seems in better spirits, but Anette says he was unable to stand when they discovered his condition.

She wants to put a spell on the girlfriend for not taking care of the elderly gentleman. She also wants a spell for good health so that she and her family can enjoy the benefits of feeling good most of the time.

As for the spell for the girlfriend, here it is:

Take a scalpel (which is a sharp knife used by surgeons) and cut a slice of lemon with it. Put the lemon in a blender with some milk and an egg. Mix well. While doing this chant:

> *Your lemon wizen you up,*
> *Egg break your head,*
> *Milk suckle your breast dry.*
> *Illness come your way*
> *For harming* [mention the victim's name].

This mixture should be served to the offending girlfriend or whoever you're putting it on. They should fall ill in a matter of days.

Now to the spell for good health. This should be done in a clean room that has been dusted and the floor thoroughly washed or vacuumed.

Take a blue candle and set it on the floor in the clean room. Take some herbs (rue, rosemary, and thyme) and burn them in the candle flame. While doing this, chant the following spell:

> *Good health come to me,*
> *Stay with me,*
> *Be always with me.*
> *Good health come to* [mention the person's name]
> *Stay with* [him/her], *be always with* [him/her].
>
> *Herbs that I burn,*
> *Cleanse the house of evil spirits*
> *And take away sickness.*
> *Be free of illness,*
> *Here in this house.*

Doing this spell will cleanse your house of germs that might otherwise attack you. Wear a mask when cleaning the room, however, so as not to stir up bacteria in your face.

You should enjoy good health indefinitely. If you've been ill or had someone in the house who was ill, this ceremony should purge the premises.

As for Anette, I recommend that she do this spell for her house as the elderly live there and are more susceptible to disease.

### To Help Raise Money

Rhonda is a reader of mine who has a friend with severe diabetes. He needs a new pancreas and the operation alone for the procedure is $150,000. She can't bear to have him bedridden the rest of his life with both legs amputated as would be the case without the transplant.

The friend is a very sweet, gentle man and is extremely kind to all he meets. He's raised about $25,000 toward the operation but needs another $125,000. This seems an insurmountable figure when you're starting from scratch.

The drugs to suppress his immune system that he'll need to take the rest of his life are costly, too, so he needs a great deal of money to get well.

Another terrible thing that's happened to the man is that his wife divorced him and has turned their daughter against him. He just doesn't have any luck. It's a case of the rich get richer and the poor get poorer. Those who are blessed receive more blessings, it seems, and those who aren't have bad luck. Why this should be is a mystery of life, but it's all cause and effect somehow. What happens to us seems to fall under that principle.

So let's fund-raise for Rhonda's friend. We need a spell

that will help him to raise money from strangers. I'm sure he's asked everyone he knows for help, and that's where he got the $25,000. Now he needs the help of deep pockets out there.

Take a diamond ring, male or female, and put it on a white taper candle. Let the wax melt down to almost the point where the ring is, then chant over it:

> *Diamond, make diamonds grow,*
> *Make money come this way,*
> *Bring money to* [mention who it's for]
> *To* [mention what it's for].
>
> *Diamond, make money.*
> *Shower me and mine,*
> *And grow for me here.*

Then blow out the candle and take the diamond off the taper. Wear it, or have your man wear it, for a week. Then do the same ceremony again, this time chanting:

> *Diamond, bring diamonds to me*
> *In the form of money*
> *For* [mention the person's name] *for* [mention what it's for].
> *Don't hide from me,*
> *And let strangers give to me*
> *So that we may have enough for* [mention what it's for].

The money should start rolling in within a few weeks if you've done the spell properly. Concentrate on hundred dollar bills when chanting the spell. You should have good fortune in a short time.

### *To Get Someone to Call*

I went for an interview some years ago and was told that the person would call me in a day or so to let me know the result of my application. So I waited around for a day and a half and then I became too anxious to let nature take its course. I resorted to witchcraft and the interviewer called me within ten minutes of me doing the spell.

Linea, a friend of mine, had a boyfriend with whom she was very much in love. They had been going together for two years when they had a terrible argument one night. Linea wanted the boyfriend to call her to apologize, so she did the spell and he called within three hours. They're going to be married in a few weeks.

Jonathan had a friend who tried to commit suicide. A mutual friend was calling everyone to let them know his condition at the hospital. Jonathan couldn't wait for his friend to call him—he wanted to know right away. So he used the spell.

These are all good examples of when it's necessary to use the spell to get someone to call you. When you're in dire need of an answer to a question and you just can't be patient but you don't want to make a nuisance of yourself by calling the person, use this spell. There's a subtle power play in phone calls. If you're the person who receives the call, then you have the upper hand in the situation. In witchcraft, there's nothing more important than having the upper hand!

All of life is a power play in one form or another. All relationships are based on the give and take of the power of one or another of you at the time. In the male-female relationship there is the one who wears the pants and the one who wears the dress. If the female is more powerful, then the relationship is lopsided and the female is probably unhappy. Women need to feel that their mates are strong and virile and intellectually their equals. If this doesn't happen, then there's a lack of respect that comes into play that makes for unhappiness.

But to get someone to call you on the phone, or to contact you on the Internet, is the question here. Whatever the location of the call (the phone or computer), take a crystal that you've bought at an occult shop and put it near the object of your call.

Chant over the crystal:

> *Contact me now,* [mention the person's name],
> *So that I may speak with you*
> *And find out about* [mention the situation you*
>     *want to know about].
> *Contact me now and don't delay*
> *I can't wait around all day.*

You should hear from the person in anywhere from ten minutes to several hours. Don't forget to visualize the person whom you want to call and send waves of love toward the image.

### *Getting Rid of Bad Habits*

Jane works for a man who farts. He comes out to her desk and does this as he gives her instructions on what to input in her computer. His office smells bad, and she is so grossed out that she doesn't know what to do. I told her she's his office wife and that he feels comfortable enough around her to do this. I tried to put the best face on it, but that doesn't cut any ice with Jane. She thinks it's so disgusting that she is looking for another job and would have been long gone if the market for jobs weren't so tight.

Wendy works for a man who picks his nose in public and leaves residue on papers that he gives her to handle.

Once she took some red pencil, circled the offending material, and asked him what it was. He was embarrassed, and got mad, and said he didn't know what it was; but he stopped doing it for awhile. Then he started up again. She wants to quit her job, too, and would if the job market were better.

I know someone who saves everything. This includes plastic bags from the vegetables in the grocery store, the bags the groceries come in, and empty glass jars and cardboard boxes. Everything you can imagine. He patrols the trash rooms in his apartment building to pick up items for his "boutique." If there's a broken lamp, he takes it and says he'll fix it. Of course it never gets fixed but is just added to the pile of things he saves.

What to do about these bad habits?! We need a spell, that's what. A bad habit can be broken with a little concentration, or if the person won't comply, then a spell will do the trick.

This kind of situation needs a guffah bag. It has to be a spell that will work for a while, so get a cloth of blue cotton, and tie it with blue cotton thread. Inside put a bullet, a sprinkle of powder, and a penny with a hole in it. Add a peacock feather if you have one or part of one on hand. Now chant over the guffah bag.

> *Habits of steel,*
> *Habits of iron,*
> *Break bad habits,*
> *Leave me alone.*

> *Let* [mention his name]*'s habits be broken*
> *And new ones appear*
> *That are good and clean.*

> *Leave me, bad habits*

*That belong to* [mention his name].
*Leave me alone and in peace.*

Concentrate on the person whose bad habits you want broken and send waves of love to his image in your mind's eye. Do this once a week for three weeks over the guffah bag, and carry it with you or wear it throughout this period. At the end of three weeks, the bad habits should begin to disappear. If they don't, then continue the spell for another three weeks. It should help by then.

## To Lose Weight

Donna is a very big-chested woman who has about sixty extra pounds on her. She's the dearest person in the world and extremely funny. She was telling me about the time she ran into her girlfriend from high school who has a master's degree, a fast-track career, a thin gorgeous body, and nicely done hair. She also has false fingernails, of course. You can just picture her and my frumpy friend meeting.

"Well, Donna, what happened to you? You used to be thin!"

"A husband and a child, that's what happened."

"But you were so hot! And look at those pounds! Is that hair real? It can't be. Let me just take a look."

Donna scrambles the imaginary girl's hair in the air.

She needs a spell to get thin, that's all there is to it.

And then there's the case of Little Mary (her mother is Big Mary), who is about two hundred pounds. She says she's always weighed too much, since she was a little child. Her mother believed that a woman should have some meat on her bones, but that doesn't go along with the cultural bias for thinness that we heavier people have to go through.

A lot of people put on weight (I know I did) when they give up smoking. Suddenly, the craving for sugar takes over, and forty pounds later there's nothing that can be done about it. Exercise helps somewhat but tends to maintain the weight. Eating small amounts just helps to lose a few pounds.

It's very discouraging and I've given up in spite of the spell that I know works, because I used it once and lost forty pounds.

But I gained it all back again by eating normal amounts of healthy food. But to lose and keep the weight off, I can only eat a small lunch, a regular dinner (albeit small), and no breakfast. This regime gets to be too much over time.

For those of you who are dedicated to getting slim and staying that way, more power to you. Here's the spell that will help you lose the weight.

Get yourself a plain gold medallion. (Tiffany's used to sell them; they're round and plain. I would think any good jewelry store might have them or could order one for you.) Have engraved on it the likeness of a fish.

Chant over the engraved medallion:

> *Golden fish, I wear you*
> *In the belief that you will make me*
> *Thin and beautiful.*
> *Curb my eating*
> *And let me eat fish and good food*
> *That will make me thin.*

Now wear the medallion and go on a diet. The pounds will just melt away without a struggle. It happened to me so I know it works. You just can't let the pounds sneak back on again.

## *To Win a Custody Battle*

I have known a wonderful young man for the last twelve years who is poor but very honest and God-fearing. However, he is attracted to women who work in go-go bars. His wife worked in one before she got a job at Burger King and started a new way of life. Now she's trying to become a teacher's aide. This woman had a child named Patricia who was hard to handle. John adopted this girl when he married the mother.

The woman and John separated, and Patricia wanted to go live with a woman named Liz to get her life together. Liz needed temporary custody to enroll her in school and such, so this was arranged. Then Liz set about trying to get permanent custody of the girl behind the mother's and John's backs. She filed a custody suit in court that they found out about accidentally through the mother's sister who was a friend of Liz.

John and his wife were stunned by the news and had to hire a lawyer to refute the case. A stranger can institute custody battles in the District of Columbia. So the woman, Liz, upped the ante. She started telling everyone that Patricia had told her she had been sexually abused—that John had been fondling her. This was completely untrue; the girl didn't even know the charges had been made against her adopted father.

Now the father and daughter will each have to testify in court about the charges. Naturally, John is very upset and in need of a spell to win custody of his child.

I recommend Obeah for this kind of situation, and a guffah bag is the surest way to ensure the witchcraft works. What you must do is get an ounce weight from a scale, ten grains of sand, a sprinkle of powder, and a fingernail from your hand (left ring finger). Put them all in a black silk guffah bag with a black satin ribbon around the top.

Chant over the guffah bag as you put it together:

*Child become mine,*
*Cleave to no other,*
*Be my baby forevermore,*
*And take no other as a mother* [or father].
*Let me win this lawsuit*
*to keep you as my own.*
*Against the odds*
*Let me hold you forever.*
*You're my heart's child,*
*And I want to be your mother* [or father].

Now carry the guffah bag around your waist until the lawsuit is complete. You should have no trouble holding on to your child if you picture your child as you make the guffah bag and send waves of love to the image you conjure.

## *To Be Popular*

A complicated situation arose at school for one of my young readers. She says that at fifteen a new boy came to her class from another school. Her best friend, Melinda, fell for him like a ton of bricks. She decided she wanted to help Melinda get him, so she did some witchcraft and it worked. He was attracted to Melinda and they started dating.

Unfortunately, after about three months of dating, the new boy came to my reader and told her he wasn't in love with Melinda and wanted to break up with her. My reader was distraught because she thought this was the ideal relationship.

Should she tell Melinda or not? She opted not to but warned her to be careful. So when he broke up with her, Melinda was heartbroken but not as surprised as she might have been.

My reader found out that the boy had used Melinda and herself to become popular at his new school. These girls were the popular ones, and he wanted to be in their set. So he told Melinda he loved her just so he could become one of them.

When the girls found this out, they were livid. They wanted to hurt this boy a lot. He has an ego problem and only loves himself, and Lord help anyone who gets in the way of his being the leader.

So Melinda and my reader want a spell to be even more popular so that they can leave this boy behind. They've already warned people in their group about him, but they want the whole school to shun him. They figure they can do this by becoming the most popular kids in school so people will listen to them.

A spell to become popular is rather hard to do. The attraction has to be from yourself to others, so you must do the spell on yourself.

Make a guffah bag. In it put a magnet, a white feather, a sprinkle of powder, and a diamond ring. (You may have to borrow one if you don't own one.)

Chant over the guffah bag as you make it of white silk with a silk thread around the top:

> *Be drawn to me,*
> *O people, be drawn to me,*
> *And feel my power.*
> *Be drawn to me, O people, be drawn to me.*
> *This is my shining hour.*
> *Popularity come to me,*
> *Make me full of imagination,*
> *Make me strong and healthy and virile,*
> *Make friends for me.*
> *Be drawn to me, O people.*

Wear the guffah bag for a month until the next full moon. Then put it in your underwear drawer or in your locker at school. Your popularity should start increasing at once and keep up the pace as you wear the guffah bag. Return the diamond after a month and a half of using it.

### *To Get the Truth*

I know a man who wants to know if his wife is having an affair with another man. He's very suspicious of her boss and thinks they've been having an affair for some time now, but he can't prove it and is at his wit's end with jealousy.

Jealousy is a terrible emotion. I've felt it a lot in my life, and I can attest to its deadly qualities. Jim, my friend, isn't at all jealous, so he's very secure. But if a woman flirts with him, you'll find me cozying up to her and interfering. I feel jealousy.

So I sympathize with anyone who has this condition and know what it does to your insides. I'm sympathetic to this man who wants to find out if his wife is carrying on an affair.

I know the wife, too, and I wouldn't put it past her as I think she's unprincipled. She's very selfish and wants only what's good for her. She isn't stingy, but she's selfish, like the young sometimes are, and she could very well be having an affair to get ahead.

So the answer, in witchcraft, for a woman who is cheating is to feed her a fried mockingbird egg. Say over the egg as you're frying it:

> *Tell me the truth,*
> *Tell until it hurts,*
> *Whether or not you're cheating,*
> *Or just a flirt.*

The mockingbird egg can be added to a drink, if you don't think frying it will do the trick. But the moment she eats the egg, she will tell the truth.

### For Suicidal Thoughts

Elaine wrote me that she is having suicidal thoughts. It happened to her grandmother, who had migraine headaches after the age of fifty, and she could find no relief from them. She finally took her own life. Elaine has inherited the migraine headaches and has had similar suicidal thoughts. She wants to know if witchcraft can cure the pain.

Sandra recently lost a boyfriend with whom she was very much in love. He died in a car accident. She has had suicidal thoughts ever since and is in very bad condition. In her case, I would recommend going to a psychiatrist to see about anti-depressant pills. There are so many drugs out these days that can help you through bad patches that it's foolish not to use them when it's necessary.

I don't think Elaine could use antidepressants, though she might be able to. Her thoughts are based on physical pain. She needs non-narcotic pain killers to get her through her migraines.

May has lost her husband. He has divorced her and taken the children. She's very depressed and needs witchcraft to help her out. She needs to go to Alcoholics Anonymous and get proper medical treatment for her depression. Alcohol induces depression, so perhaps if she stopped drinking and taking drugs the depression would vanish.

In all cases the cure for depression is a visit to a good psychiatrist who can assess the situation and prescribe for it. But it sometimes takes two or three weeks for anti-depressant pills to work, so it doesn't hurt to have a little witchcraft working for you during the interim.

Make a guffah bag with a silver coin, a red feather, a piece of net (hairnet will do), and some powder. Wrap these items in a pink silk cloth and use pink silk thread to close it. As you're making the guffah bag, chant:

> *Sadness go away, leave me be.*
> *Let suicidal thoughts leave me.*
> *Bring sunshine and happiness to me.*
>
> *Let me be free*
> *Of sadness and fear.*
> *And please, God,*
> *My prayer hear.*
>
> *Sadness go away, leave me be.*
> *Let suicidal thoughts leave me.*

Wear the guffah bag until the suicidal thoughts stop. This should be in a matter of days, sometimes hours.

While chanting, picture yourself in a happy state of mind, with a smile on your face. Send waves of love to this mental image of yourself.

### For Creativity

I have heard from a New Age musician who wants his creative juices to flow into musical spaces. This gives me an opportunity to talk about creativity.

Creativity comes from a deep wellspring within us and is set free at our fingertips or our lips (if we sing). It's a gift from God and is nurtured or aborted in childhood, like so many of our permanent characteristics are. If it's nurtured, then we become creative as we get older. But if it's aborted, then we take up knitting, or something, as a substitute. I'm not saying that knitting isn't creative because it is, but we change our creative patterns to something that isn't what we might have been.

There is a lot of fear with creativity. Getting ready for a performance on the typewriter or at the piano involves overcoming fear that we'll fail and sitting down to do it anyway. You're really kind of a soldier when you can be actively creative, as soldiers have to face down fear too.

The voice that is our own speaks the words that we write or sing or play. And we must learn to trust this voice—that it won't let us down. All of this takes maturity and overcoming odds to accomplish. That's why creative artists are valued so highly. They've fought a battle with themselves and won.

To nurture yourself into the creative mode, there is a spell that will help. It follows:

Take a white candle and set it in the middle of a darkened room. Put by it the artifacts of your creativity. A fountain pen, if you're a writer; a sheet of music if you're a musician or singer. Then put your picture close to it.

Concentrate on your picture and say the following chant:

> *Creativity flow from me,*
> *Come to me in the quiet of the night.*
> *Flow from my fingertips* [or lips]
> *And make me brilliant.*
> *Let me write* [or sing or play] *with*
> *inspiration.*
>
> *Creativity flow from me.*
> *Come from God and set me free.*

Don't forget to light the candle before you chant and conjure a huge amount of love in your heart. Let the image of yourself being creative flow to your head, and let the emotion of love overwhelm you there.

Love is the wellspring of all creativity, and you must be a loving person to be creative. You give of yourself in the process, and that's why the gifts of creativity and love come from God.

### *To Get What You Want*

Madeline, who is eighteen, wants a forty-one-year-old man. I don't think she should but she wants him with all of her heart. Maybe I should help her.

Jeanne wants a new job. It's very hard to get a job here in Washington, but she wants one anyway. She's tired of her current job and would like to be in new surroundings. I think I should help her get a new job.

Carey wants to leave her husband and move to Colorado. She has a boyfriend there and wants to start life over with him. She would take her daughter with her from a former marriage, but leave her husband and his kids behind. I really don't think I should help her, but that's what she wants, so what can I do?

Beth wants a fence in her back yard so she can have a puppy. Because fences are expensive and she wants the money to put one up, I think I can help her. This sounds harmless enough.

Jeremy wants to get off his medications and live a normal life. He's schizophrenic and needs the medication for his condition, but it's making his hands and feet shake. I don't think witchcraft as I'm describing it can cure mental illness. (You'd have to go to a Hawaiian or African witchdoctor to do that. But I can help Jeremy come to an idea about what he should do.

Samantha wants to be rich. She's an actress and is in

the business for acquiring wealth so it's possible she can get what she wants. This spell will help her.

The following spell is to get what you want. Be careful in asking for this, however, because what you want isn't always good for you.

You may wish for a man who's forty-one when you're eighteen, but that doesn't mean that this is the best decision of your life. In particular, since Madeline comes from a small town and basically wants to get out of it, she'll choose any route to get away.

And Carey leaving her husband is being selfish. She's thinking only of her own happiness. What about him? What will leaving him do to him? She should stop and consider an action that might send her straight to hell.

Anyway, here is the spell to get what you want:

Take a horseshoe and put it around a red candle. Put the candle in a darkened room in the middle of a table. Write what it is you want on a piece of parchment with a quill pen dipped in black ink. Chant the following as you write:

> *What I want*
> *I write here.*
> *Please take my dream*
> *And bring it near.*
> *What I want*
> *Is what I should get.*
> *Let all my dreams*
> *Now be met.*

Now take the parchment and fold it in a square of four creases. Hold it over the candle with a pair of tweezers and let it burn. Picture yourself with your wish fulfilled as you burn the parchment. Send waves of love at the image you conjure of yourself.

## To Ward Off Evil Spirits

Evil spirits roam the earth looking for people to haunt. They have done that since the earliest times (since the Garden of Eden) and whisper evil in our ears for our hearts to hear. When you hear the temptation of evil, you must fight it at once so you'll be set free. The evil voice usually doesn't last too long, so you only have to fight it for a little while. Then the temptation passes.

Evil spirits are disembodied, but they think and take pleasure in their evil. They jump and flit through the air and land on your head and enter in that way. Some people are weaker than others and listen to the blandishments that the evil spirits offer. They promise rewards for evil, and these rewards almost always turn into punishments.

To guard against evil spirits, the use of iron is recommended by Obeah witches. Use fresh iron nails to form your initials above your door jamb. If you keep an iron-bladed knife around, too, that's a good thing to own against evil spirits.

One man swears that he staves off evil spirits by soaking his guffah bag in whiskey—and then wearing it. The evil spirits stay away, he says. Of course, this man is an alcoholic so he attributes wonders to alcohol, but you may try it if you like.

Evil spirits are to be fought constantly and daily. They have a life of their own and will gladly take your life if you let them.

Fight against evil spirits at every turn and eventually they learn to leave you alone. You'll be at peace most of the time if you fight the evil spirits.

## To Prevent the Sale of Stolen Goods

If you've ever been robbed you know what a rape the situation really is. You feel completely violated and taken advantage of. When I was robbed (all that was taken was my television), I kept feeling that the thief would come back and rob me again. So I moved within three weeks of the robbery.

I have a very good friend who was held up at knife point the other night. He was coming out of a building in a semi-bad section of Washington, when a man at a bus stop told him to back down into a stairwell and give him his wallet. My friend did so, and said later he felt he had been raped. He had never understood what women were talking about, but now he understood.

The violence associated with theft is terrible. We've had a rash of gentlemen burglars who break into rich people's homes and hold them up for small sums of money. Their pleasure in the robberies is probably the feeling of power they have over their victims right in their victim's houses. It's a sadistic type of crime that these men pull: The object is to make the people feel insecure and violated. Their very homes aren't safe.

The following Obeah spell is to be used against a thief so he can't sell the goods he's stolen:

Take a key from the drawer from where the goods were stolen and some dirt from the footprint of the thief. Tie these tightly together in a cloth and bury them by your front doorstep. If you live in an apartment, keep it by your front door. The thief will be unable to sell your stolen property and won't benefit from the theft.

## To Guard Against Spells

One of my young readers wrote to say that he was bewitched with a spell and overcame it by using a spell from one of my books. Someone put a spell on him to give him a stomach ache, and it was excruciating until he held a tiger's eye stone in his hand and chanted to get the spell off him. It went away immediately and did not return, so it was definitely a spell someone had put on him.

A young woman of my acquaintance had also been bewitched. A friend whose boyfriend she took put a spell on her (understandably so, I think) that consisted of her not being able to have an orgasm. It worked so well she was going crazy until I broke the spell.

Another reader wrote to say that his mother-in-law had a crush on him and had put a spell on her daughter, his wife. The girl was unable to get pregnant, and when the spell was lifted she became pregnant almost overnight.

There's the old story of jealousy—keeping a young woman from a man the other woman wanted. She put a spell on the young woman, causing her to have a car accident.

A maid didn't want her boss to move out of town and throw her out of work, so she put a spell on him to stay. When all of his plans fell through, he discovered the spell on him and had it removed.

The amulet to carry to keep spells away is the hairball in the stomach of a cow. You can ask a butcher to save you one, and then carry it as an amulet against harm from spells.

### To Keep Violence Away

In this day of gun-toting people on the highways and the streets, violence is never far away. Even if you, like me, confine your activities to daylight hours, there is every chance a bank robbery or some other violence with gangs will occur on the streets. People are always being robbed, and it behooves you to carry an amulet against violence.

A young woman was murdered the other day by her

live-in boyfriend. This is always happening in Washington. She made him mad about something and he took her life. You just can't afford to make people angry these days. They're not above killing you.

Of course, one way to ward off violence is to carry a can of Mace. I used to do that until I tried using it once for practice and the wind blew it back in my face. You should have seen me run down the street for the nearest restaurant where I could find a basin of water to bathe my face in! Was I a mess! That's the last time I carried a can of Mace to protect against harm. Now I'm just very careful.

Rape is a violent crime that women are always in fear of. I knew a girl who was in Acapulco on vacation when a beachbum swam with her out in the deep water, took off her bikini bottom, and raped her in the water. There was absolutely nothing she could do about it because he said he'd drown her if she didn't cooperate.

The amulet to carry against violence is an Obeah one: Three grains of corn and a crab claw tied in a bit of black cloth will keep violence away. You may also use bandanna cloth if you have that.

### Perfume for Garments

One of the great pleasures of life is perfume. It brightens every occasion and brings good feelings about life in general to the wearer.

Never have perfumes been as prevalent as they are today, and they have been improved so the perfume scent keeps going over a long period of time. When you buy traditional perfume, it is almost a relief that it doesn't last as long as some of the newer ones.

One girl at our office wears the same long-lasting perfume every day. She lights up the ladies room, the hallways, her work area, and mine when she draws near. It's almost too much perfume to bear. She must bathe herself in it every morning.

But the old-fashioned Obeah way to scent yourself and your clothing is with moss. Moss bags and moss balls are made into amulets or sachets then worn on the body and put in among the clothes in the closet. It wards off evil spirits as well as acting as a scent, and we can all use help with evil spirits when we can get it.

### To Ward Off Ghosts

I was in the living room of an inn on Vieques Island off Puerto Rico, talking to a witch friend, and she said, "there's a ghost in here." I looked, and sure enough I saw a wisp of white hovering by the mantlepiece. Since then, I've looked for ghosts and have seen them again.

I was in my apartment in New York when I saw my second ghost. He was a tall black man and he walked right by me in my apartment. The girl down the hall had seen him, too. He was just an impression of black air, but he was definitely there. He brushed past me, and I felt the wind from his passing.

But there are more than ghosts that we must watch out for. There are goblins, haunts, specters, spirits, apparitions, and Jack-o'-lanterns. These are the definition of the Obeah witches whom I use as source material for most of this book.

If you've ever seen a ghost you know how apprehensive you become. What will it do? Probably nothing put pass through. But there are tales of poltergeists who rip up homes with their antics.

The amulet to wear to ward off ghosts, apparitions, and all other forms of materialization is made of alligator teeth. You should try to procure some of these by writing to alligator farms in Florida. They may have some on hand to sell or give away. These teeth are also mana for problems with the throat or neck, but they're most useful in keeping away ghosts. They can also attract powerful good luck, so they're an all-around good amulet to acquire.

### For Depression

Depression leads to suicide if left unchecked. It's a leading cause of death. I have it, so I know what I'm talking about. But I also have the cure.

I take Prozac, which I just started taking, and I haven't noticed a tremendous difference, so my doctor will have to adjust the dosage. This is one defense against depression.

Depression makes you feel as if nothing is any good. It makes you feel like you dislike people and you don't want to do anything. It's like your whole personality is colored by this disease. There's no disgrace to depression, it just is, and it must be dealt with.

I discovered, riding on the bus, a defense against depression. I noticed that the Prozac was working a little bit and I suddenly felt good and discovered it was because I felt excitement and love in my heart. Actual love was coming from my heart organ, and it spread through my body and made me feel good. So I recommend that if you're depressed, you should actively feel love and it will make you feel good. Then I think of Jim, my companion, and how he's never depressed. It's because he always feels love; he operates on love. I don't know why, after twenty years, I never analyzed it before, but the reason he's never depressed is because he feels love. That's the key to overcoming depression. When you don't feel anything, the vacuum is filled up with morose feelings. You must actively participate in your happiness and in feeling good.

There's also a witchcraft spell for depression.

Take rose petals, jonquil petals, and cherry blossoms, if you can get them, and spread them all over the carpet of your living room.

Take off your shoes and run around in the petals as you chant:

> *Leave me, bad feeling,*
> *Leave me alone.*
> *Let me sing in the wind,*
> *Let me play in the day.*
> *Let me know happiness,*
> *Let me know love,*
> *Let me know peace and joy,*
> *And let me be free.*
> *Freedom is love.*
> *Let me feel love.*

Now light a candle and put a diamond ring on your left ring finger. Chant the chant again while staring into the candle and picturing yourself as free from depression.

Your depression should start lifting almost at once. Probably running through the petals will lift it, but definitely marrying happiness will do it. Feel love in your heart, and you'll know boundless joy. You'll want to do things and help people and feel good all the time.

Depression is a killer disease. Don't fool with it. If the spell doesn't lift the feelings you have, and the love doesn't work full time, take a modern-day miracle drug for it. Suicide is never far away as an option for the depressed, and therefore the feeling must be avoided.

### To Assess Guilt

I know a girl who lies about nearly everything. She has a job where she shouldn't lie because her actions are visible, but she does so anyway. She once lied about me. I got even with her by lying about her. (Not very mature, but effective.)

But when someone lies and you want to know the truth, there's an Obeah way to find out. Say a man is accused of stealing. He should have some recourse if he's innocent, and the Obeah trick is a way to find out if he's truly innocent, guilty as sin, or knows something about the crime.

I know a man whose mother had an affair with a married man; he was the resulting child of that union. The wife of the married man was so angry that she put a spell on the child that he would almost grasp success in life but then have it taken away. She went to a witchwoman in Mexico to have this spell done. (My friend is Mexican.) My friend became a movie director in Mexico and his pictures met with success, but he didn't. He's now driving a cab for a living and is poor.

This story really grabs me because this man was an innocent child when the spell was put on him. He had no control over who he was or what the circumstances of his birth were. The victim of the spell should have been his mother for having an affair with another woman's husband, but the wife was definitely out to get this woman, and getting the child seemed the best way. I don't recommend this method; you must be careful of what you do in witchcraft so you won't wind up in hell.

Now the spell to tell if someone is guilty is somewhat complex. It should be done in the company of others, if possible, and especially the person you're testing, if he or she can be brought into the picture.

Take a sifter (a sieve or a flour sifter will do). Put it between two chairs and rest it so it will easily fall, so a breath would dislodge it. Then, with uplifted hands, start the following incantation:

*By the God who made us all,*
*Sifter, sifter, stand or fall.*
*Come up, Peter; come up, Paul.*
*Now you sifter, stand or fall.*

*By St. Peter, by St. Paul,*
*By the good Lord who made us all,*
*If* [mention the person's name] *did* [mention the deed],
*Turn, sifter, turn and fall.*

If the person accused is innocent, the sifter will remain motionless. If she has guilty knowledge, the sifter will shake. If she is the culprit, it slowly turns and falls toward the chanter.

As you can see, this is an Obeah spell with power. It comes straight from the country and should best be done in the country. But if you're a city witch, just make sure you put the sifter between the chairs so just a breath of air will turn it. Make sure no one stamps his foot or blows on it to make it fall.

# Ƕow Ⱳⱦcȟcȓⱥfⱦ Ƕⱥs Ƕelpeⱥ Ⱳe

I'VE NEVER PUT DOWN in words before now how witchcraft has actually helped me in my life. But one of my readers wants to know, so I figure it's a legitimate question.

Let me tell you the kind of life I lead. I go to work every day and have a good job. I get in early, around seven, so I can be away from the office around 3:30. During the week I come home, take a nap, and have dinner, then write for an hour or so. Then I watch television with Jim, my companion of twenty years, and we drift off to sleep when we're tired. On the weekends I have a very nice social life. I belong to the National Society of American Pen Woman, the Daughters of the American Revolution, and the Washington Concert Opera group, and I go to all their functions. I also have a circle of friends I do things with—like have lunches out—and Jim and I do things together.

So I live a busy, full, rich life.

It was not always this way. Before witchcraft, I did not have Jim in my life, and I bounced around from pillar to post. I had a lot of fun but I just wasn't fulfilled. When I met Jim, my life began to calm down, and I took on the trappings of a full, rich life. In my thirties I lived in New

York, suddenly got tired of that, left my job, and moved to Tahiti and Hawaii. I did a geographic cure for my lack of having a wonderful man in my life.

I was very unhappy without the appropriate mate. I didn't want to just live life for myself, I wanted to share my life with someone wonderful. Jim is that wonderful man. He allows me to be free and do as I want to do without jealousy (I have male friends too in my circle with whom I lunch). Jim encourages me and gets me started on projects when I get lazy or tired. We genuinely love each other and tell each other often of our feelings. We've been in love for twenty years, and it gets better all the time. (I keep having to say twenty years because it has gone by in a flash.)

The secret to a happy life is to have someone wonderful to share it with. If you find the right man, and hold out for him, you will be rewarded with great happiness. Witchcraft can help you achieve this.

Here's the spell I used to find Jim.

Take a white candle and a needle. Sit in a dark room before the candle and put the needle through the wick. Then light it and let the flame burn down to the needle before you blow out the candle. Chant over the candle the following spell:

> *Oh Power, if there be a power,*
> *Hear my prayer to thee.*
> *Bring a man who loves me to me,*
> *And a man I can love in return.*
> *Bring happiness and great joy to my life,*
> *And I will pray to you always with thanksgiving.*

Within two weeks of doing that spell I met Jim. He has been the source of inspiration to me in my life.